NIUBI!

The Real Chinese You Were Never Taught in School

牛 **niú** (*nyoo*) awesome
酷 **kù** (*coo*) cool
他妈的 **tāmāde** (*tah mah duh*) damn
我操 **wǒ cào** (*wuh tsow*) fuck!
屄 **bī** (*bee*) pussy

EVELINE CHAO is a freelance writer and editor based in Beijing. She is extremely fortunate to have foul-mouthed friends willing to teach her words that most Chinese would be too embarrassed to reveal to a foreigner.

NIUBI!

The Real Chinese You Were
Never Taught in School

EVELINE CHAO

Illustrations by Chris Murphy

A PLUME BOOK

PLUME
Published by Penguin Group
Penguin Group (USA) Inc., 375 Hudson Street, New York, New York 10014, U.S.A. •
Penguin Group (Canada), 90 Eglinton Avenue East, Suite 700, Toronto, Ontario,
Canada M4P 2Y3 (a division of Pearson Penguin Canada Inc.) • Penguin Books Ltd., 80
Strand, London WC2R 0RL, England • Penguin Ireland, 25 St. Stephen's Green, Dublin 2,
Ireland (a division of Penguin Books Ltd.) • Penguin Group (Australia), 250 Camberwell
Road, Camberwell, Victoria 3124, Australia (a division of Pearson Australia Group Pty.
Ltd.) • Penguin Books India Pvt. Ltd., 11 Community Centre, Panchsheel Park, New
Delhi – 110 017, India • Penguin Books (NZ), 67 Apollo Drive, Rosedale, North Shore
0632, New Zealand (a division of Pearson New Zealand Ltd.) • Penguin Books (South
Africa) (Pty.) Ltd., 24 Sturdee Avenue, Rosebank, Johannesburg 2196, South Africa

Penguin Books Ltd., Registered Offices: 80 Strand, London WC2R 0RL, England

First published by Plume, a member of Penguin Group (USA) Inc.

First Printing, December 2009
10 9 8 7 6 5 4 3 2 1

Copyright © Eveline Chao, 2009
Illustrations by Chris Murphy
All rights reserved

LIBRARY OF CONGRESS CATALOGING-IN-PUBLICATION DATA
Chao, Eveline.
  Niubi! : the real Chinese you were never taught in a school / Eveline Chao;
Illustrations by Chris Murphy.
    p. cm.
  ISBN 978-0-452-29556-8
  1. Chinese language—Conversation and phrase books—English. 2. Chinese
language—Spoken Chinese—Dictionaries—English. 3. Language and culture—
China. 4. China—Languages. I. Title.
  PL1125.E6C383 2009
  495.1'83421—dc22

                                                                    009028618

Printed in the United States of America

Contents

Acknowledgments

Endless thanks first and foremost to Maya Rock for making it all happen. I am also grateful to my agent Al Zuckerman at Writers House and my editor Nadia Kashper at Plume. Chris Murphy deserves special mention for his wonderful illustrations. And finally, thanks to Lu Bin, Amani Zhang, Wang Bin, Rachel Zhu, Emilio Liu, Lisa Hsia, Sam Zhao of *les+* magazine, and Cecilia Hu, Gissing Liu, and Vivid Zhu for their advice and help on this project.

Introduction

On my first day in Beijing, my roommate and old college friend Ann sent me off to IKEA with three of her best Chinese friends. They picked me up in a red Volkswagen Santana and passed around a joint, blasting the Cure and Sonic Youth the whole ride there. In the crowded cafeteria at IKEA, we ate Swedish meatballs, french fries, and kung pao chicken, and then skated around the store with our shopping carts, stepping over the snoring husbands, asleep on the display couches, and smiling at the peasant families taking family photos in the living room sets. I bought bedding and some things for the kitchen, Da Li got a couple of plants, and Wang Xin bought a lamp. Traffic was bad on the ride home; we were navigating through a snarl at an intersection when yet another car cut us off. Lu Bin stuck his head out the window and bellowed "傻屄!" "**Shǎbī!**" (*shah bee*), or "fucking cunt," at the other driver, then placidly turned down the music and, looking back, asked if I was a fan of Nabokov—he'd read *Lolita* in the Chinese translation and it was his favorite book.

For the next few months, I was too terrified to leave the apartment by myself and go make other friends, having not yet fully absorbed the fact that I'd left behind four years of life and a career in New York City and suddenly moved to this new and crazy place. So with a few exceptions, those three boys and my roommate were the only people I hung out with. Da Li owned an Italian restaurant, of all things, and we'd often meet there late in the evening and eat crème brûlée or drink red wine or consume whatever else we could beg off of him for free, and then pile into his and Lu Bin's cars and head out on whatever adventure they had in mind. One night some big DJ from London was in town, spinning at a multilevel megaclub filled with nouveau riche Chinese. I bounced around on the metal trampoline dance floor and learned that the big club drink in China is whiskey with sweet green tea. Another night we headed to a smoke-filled dive to see a jazz band. The keyboardist had gone to high school with Lu Bin in Beijing, studied jazz in New York, and now sometimes performed with Cui Jian, a rock performer whose music, now banned from state radio, served as an unofficial anthem for the democracy movement during the late 1980s. My friends had a party promoter friend—a tiny, innocuous-seeming girl—who somehow got us into everything for free and would always turn and grin after rocking out to a set by a death-metal band from Finland, or a local hip-hop crew, and shout out, "太牛屄!" "**Tài niúbī!**" (*tie nyoo bee*), or "That was fucking awesome!" Other nights the boys would want to drive all the way to the Korean part of town, just to try out some Korean BBQ joint they'd heard about. And some nights we'd just drive around aimlessly and 岔 **chǎ** (*chah*), Beijing slang for "shoot the shit," about music or art. Then we'd go back to Lu Bin's to drink beer and watch DVDs (pirated, of course).

Most nights ended with deciding to get food at four in the morning and driving to Ghost Street, an all-night strip of restaurants lit up with red lanterns. There was one hot pot restaurant in particular that they liked, where, I remember, one night a screaming match broke out between two drunk girls at a table near ours. It concluded with one girl jumping up and shouting, "操你妈!" "**Cào nǐ mā!**" (*tsow nee ma*), or "Fuck you!" before storming out the door. The bleary-looking man left behind tried to console the other bawling girl, assuring her, "没事，她喝醉了" "**Méishì, tā hēzuì le**" (*may shih, tah huh dzway luh*): "Don't worry about it—she was totally wasted."

Intermittently, some new girl, whom one of the boys had recently decided was the love of his life, would appear in the group. There was a comic period when Da Li, who couldn't speak any English, was 收 **shōu** (*show*), or screwing, a tall blonde who couldn't speak any Chinese. Whenever they came out, one of us would inevitably get roped into playing translator in the long lead-up to the moment when they would finally leave us to go back to his place. You'd always get stuck repeating, over and over, some trivial thing that one had said to the other, and which the other was fixating on, thinking something important had been said. "What'd she say again?" Da Li would shout over the noise of the bar. "酷" "**Kù**" (*coo*), I'd yell back: "cool" in Chinese.

After a couple of years here, I've started taking Beijing for granted, and it's harder for me to conjure up the same sense of magic and wonderment I felt at every little detail during those first few months. But then I'll go back home, for a visit, to the United States and be reminded by the questions I'm asked of what a dark and mysterious abstraction China remains for most of the world. "Does everyone ride bicycles?" "Are there drugs in China?" "What are Chinese curse words like?" "Is there a hook-up scene? What's dating like in China?" "What's it like to be gay in China? Is it awful?" "How do you type Chinese on a computer? Are the keyboards different?" "How do Chinese URLs work?" One guy even asked, in gape-jawed amazement, if outsiders were allowed into the country.

Every time I hear these questions, I think back to those three boys who so strongly shaped my first impressions of China and wish that everyone could share the experiences I had—experiences that were neither "Western," as half the people I talk to seem to expect, nor "Chinese," as the other half expects, but rather their own unique thing. And then I remember the way those boys and their friends spoke—the casual banter, the familiar tone, the many allusions to both Western pop culture and ancient Chinese history; the mockery, the cursing, the lazy stoner talk, the dirty jokes, the arguments, the cynicism, the gossip and conjectures and sex talk about who was banging whom, but most of the time just the utterly banal chatter of everyday life—and I realize that one of the best ways to understand the true realities of a culture, in all its ordinariness and remarkableness, is to know the slang and new expressions and everyday speech being said on the street.

Hopefully, then, with the words in this book, some of those questions will be answered. Are there drugs in China? There are indeed drugs and stoners and cokeheads and all the rest in China, and, contrary to popular belief, lighting up a joint doesn't instantly result in some sort of trapdoor opening in the sky and an iron-fisted authoritarian force descending from above to execute you on the spot. There's even a massive heroin problem in the country, discussed in chapter 7. What about the gay scene? There is one and it's surprisingly open, at least in the biggest cities. And I hope that after reading through the sex terms in chapter 5, the prostitution terminology in chapter 7, and the abundance of terms relating to extramarital affairs in chapter 4, we can put an end to those "exposés" about sex in China that are always appearing in the Western media, predicated on an outdated assumption that Chinese people somehow don't have sex.

The Internet, in particular, is worth a special mention for its role in spreading slang and other new words. It was the sudden appearance of Internet cafés in the 1990s, for example, that first helped popularize the concept of coolness in China. The word 酷 **kù** (*coo*), a transliteration of the English word "cool," first appeared in Hong Kong and Taiwan; young people in mainland China learned it over the Internet from their friends there and spread the term at home. By the late 1990s, **kù** was known on most college campuses across China.

Here's the thing: you can live in China forever—you can even live in China forever and speak great Chinese—and fail to notice even the merest hint of the subcultures represented by the slang in this book. For many people, the Chinese are the shy and almost absurdly innocent students in their classes, who look embarrassed at the merest mention of dating or sex; the white-collar staff who never speak up at meetings and leave their Western bosses convinced they're incapable of expressing an opinion or thinking up an original idea; the prim, strict tutors who conjure up an image of China as a land of studying machines; and the dolled-up, gold-digging girls who hang on the arms of rich men in shady bars late at night.

These impressions of China are not inaccurate—they just aren't everything. Pay just a little more attention and you'll notice a fuller array of people and have a more nuanced portrait of the life humming below the surface. You may notice that on Thursday nights this one Italian sandwich shop fills up with gay men grabbing dinner before the weekly gay night at the upscale bar around the corner, or that the old guy fixing bikes down the street is an ex-con who spent a couple of decades in prison, or that the middle-aged couple snuggling in the booth near you at that Hong Kong–style restaurant are clearly two married people having an affair, or that all the women's bathrooms are locked in this one public building nearby because there's a flasher who lurks in the neighborhood.

I have a running gag with an American friend of mine who, despite two years of living in Beijing, insists she has *never* heard a single Chinese curse word. I bombard her with text messages and e-mails every single day, itemizing every swear I hear on the street: 10:00 a.m.—middle-aged woman on bus yelling "Fuck!" into cell phone; 3:30 p.m.—two college-age guys walking behind me while standing at ATM saying, "That fucking shit was fucking ri-fucking-diculous"; 11:30 p.m.—two teenage girls in McDonald's bitching about some woman they keep referring to as "that old cunt." And every time I see her, my friend says again that she never hears anything, not a single "fuck" or "shit" or "damn." And every time, I keep insisting: "You just need to know what to hear."

How to read this book

So, how *do* Chinese keyboards work? The answer is 拼音 **pīnyīn** (*peen yeen*), literally "spell sound." A system for the romanization of Chinese words using the Latin alphabet, it was adopted in 1979 by the Chinese government. Students of Chinese as a second language start out by learning pinyin and pinyin pronunciation, as do Chinese schoolchildren. And road signs in China often depict pinyin beneath the Chinese characters.

Using pinyin, the word for "me," 我, can also be written **wǒ** (pronounced *wuh*). That symbol over the *o* is a tone mark; there are four different marks each representing one of the four different tones—first tone, second tone, third tone, and fourth tone—that may be used to pronounce each Chinese syllable. (Because it is so cumbersome to type pinyin with the tone marks in place, people often leave them out or stick the tone number behind the syllable, as in "wo3.")

Typing in Chinese is done using pinyin. It's a cumbersome process because Chinese has a huge number of homonyms. Thus, the way most character input systems work, to type 我 you type in **wo**, and then a window pops up showing the huge range of characters that are all pronounced *wuh*. You scroll through, and when you get to the right one, you hit enter and the character is typed on the screen. It's a slow process, and should you ever find yourself working an office job in China, your Chinese coworkers will be mightily impressed by how quickly you're able to type in English.

There was once a time when pinyin was a contender to replace the character-based Chinese writing system altogether, but that never really panned out, and the government settled for simplifying many notoriously hard-to-write traditional characters into what is known as simplified Chinese, the writing system used in mainland China, as opposed to traditional Chinese, which is still used in Taiwan, Macao, and Hong Kong).

The words in this book are all presented in three different ways. First I give the simplified Chinese characters for the term. Then appears the pinyin, in bold, with tone marks. Then, for those who are new to Chinese and have not yet learned pinyin, I have written out, in italics and parenthesized, the word's phonetic pronunciation (although pinyin uses the Latin alphabet, the letters do not correspond to English pronunciation, so you won't be able to pronounce pinyin without having studied it first).

As mentioned, the words in this book are all given in simplified Chinese. There are, however, a very few instances when I list a slang term that is only used in Taiwan, in which case I also give the traditional characters, since Taiwan still uses the old character system.

You'll notice that most of the terms in this book can be used throughout Mandarin-speaking China, but because I live in Beijing, words specific to Beijing and northern China in general are a bit more well-represented than southern and Taiwanese terms. However, as the capital of China, Beijing is used as the national standard and has an inordinate amount of influence; thus a great deal of Beijing slang winds up spreading throughout the country. In any case, rest assured that you won't find yourself using southern terms with an uncomprehending northerner, or vice versa, as I have taken care to indicate whenever a term is native to just one part of China.

I have also been careful to note how strong or vulgar the insults and swear words are, and to situate the words within the appropriate context. After all, we don't want to unleash, onto the unsuspecting Chinese populace, readers armed with utterly inappropriate words for inappropriate situations. With this book you won't unwittingly yell, "You poopie-head!" at the son of a bitch who grabs your ass while walking down the street or shout, "Motherfucking cunt!" when you stub your toe in front of a sweet old grandmother.

You should also be aware that many of the terms in this book are almost exclusively spoken, and never written, and thus may not have a set way of being expressed in characters—especially if the word originated out of a non-Mandarin dialect. Fortunately, the Internet has given people a reason to agree on ways to write various colloquial expressions, and so I have managed to give the most commonly used characters for every term in this book. But, especially with a few of the extremely localized words, you may find that not everyone will agree with the written form given or even know of a way to write the word.

And finally, it's worth keeping in mind that alternative subcultures haven't permeated Chinese society as thoroughly as they have in the West, where everyone knows about once-underground ideas like hip-hop and gay culture and surfers and stoners—the margins of society from which much slang is born. For this reason, entire sections of this book are filled with terminology that your average, mainstream Chinese will have never heard. At the least, you will in most cases need to be talking to someone from a certain subculture for them to know the words associated with that scene.

And now, as Chinese spectators at sports games or encouraging parents might yell, 加油! **jiāyóu!** (*jah yo*). Literally "refuel" or "add gasoline," it also means "let's go!"

CHAPTER ONE

Cow Pussy, Yes, Cow Pussy

Let's begin with . . . cow pussy. Or rather, 牛屄 **niúbī** (*nyoo bee*), which literally translates to "cow pussy" but means "fuckin' awesome" or "badass" or "really fuckin' cool." Sometimes it means something more like "big" and "powerful," and sometimes it can have the slightly more negative meaning of "bragging" or "braggart" or "being audacious," but most of the time it means "fuckin' awesome."

The etymology of **niúbī** is unknown. Some say the idea is that a cow's pussy is really big, so things that are similarly impressive are called cow cunts. Others say that it stems from the expression 吹牛皮 **chuī niúpí** (*chway nyoo pee*), which literally translates to "blow up ox hide" and also connotes bragging or a braggart (someone who can blow a lot of air). In fact, the word for bragging is the first part of that phrase, 吹牛 **chuīniú** (*chway nyoo*). Once upon a time (and you can still see this done today in countries like Pakistan), people made rafts out of animal hides that had to be blown up with air so they would float. Such an activity obviously required one mighty powerful set of lungs, and so it is thought that **niúbī** derives from **chuī niúpí** both because of the association with power and bigness and because the two expressions rhyme.

Some people merely use the shortened 牛 **niú** (*nyoo*)—that is, the cow minus the cunt—to mean "awesome" or "great." Unlike **niúbī**, saying **niú** is not really vulgar, much like saying "that sucks" instead of "that fuckin' sucks dick."

Despite its generally positive meaning, **niúbī** is a dirty, dirty word—dirty enough that the character for "pussy" or "cunt," 屄 **bī** (*bee*), was removed from the Chinese character set years ago and cannot be typed on most computers. Your average Chinese doesn't even know how to write it; others do but choose not to write the real character because it is so dirty. When people use the word **niúbī** online, they often write 牛B or NB because *N* and *B* are the first letters of the pinyin syllables **niú** and **bī**. Roman letters are frequently used in this way, as informal abbreviations of Chinese words. For example, Beijing is often abbreviated BJ, and Shanghai SH, as it is easier than typing out the Chinese characters, which can be a somewhat arduous process.

You'll also often see **niúbī** written 牛比 or 牛逼 instead of 牛屄. The characters 比 and 逼 are homonyms of 屄; they have completely different meanings but are also pronounced *bee*, and so they are used as stand-ins. Chinese has a huge number of homonyms—syllables that sound the same but have different meanings—and as you'll see with many of the terms throughout this book, this makes for a lot of wordplay and puns.

Niúbī started out as Beijing slang but has spread enough that it is fairly ubiquitous throughout the country, in particular at any event involving a large population of punk rockers, hip young Chinese, or your average, beer-drinking man. Rock shows and soccer matches are especially prime hot spots. A really hot band or a particularly impressive sports move is 太牛屄 **tài niúbī** (*tie nyoo bee*), "too fuckin' awesome," or 真牛屄 **zhēn niúbī** (*dzen nyoo bee*), "really fuckin' awesome," or—my own favorite construction—

牛屄死了**niúbī sǐ le** (*nyoo bee sih luh*), which literally translates "fuckin' awesome to the point of death."

Those last few phrases point to one of the most satisfying
things about the Chinese language: the modular way that
everything—characters, words, phrases, sentences—is constructed. In that last phrase, **niúbī sǐ le**, the individual component 死 **sǐ** (*sih*) is itself a word meaning "die" or "death."
Adding the larger component 死了**sǐ le** (*sih luh*) after an adjective is a common way of amping up the meaning of the
adjective. So we can swap out **niúbī** and plug other words
into the phrase—for example 饿 **è** (*uh*), which means "hungry." If you are 饿死了**è sǐ le** (*uh sih luh*), you are absolutely
starving; that is, "hungry to the point of death."

Almost every syllable in Chinese is itself a word, and larger words are constructed by simply linking these syllables
together. The result is a remarkably logical language in
which the components of a word often explain, very literally,
the meaning of that word. Thus a telephone is 电话 **diànhuà**
(*dyinn hwah*), literally "electric speech," and a humidifier is
加湿器 **jiāshīqì** (*jah shih chee*), literally "add wetness device."
(That said, you shouldn't get too preoccupied with the literal
meaning of every single word, as the components of a word
may also be chosen for reasons unrelated to its meaning,
such as pronunciation.)

Individual Chinese characters (that is, the symbols that
make up Chinese writing) tend to be modular as well, composed of discrete components (or "radicals") that may carry
their own meaning and that often help explain the overall
meaning of the character. The character for "pussy," 屄 **bī**
(*bee*), for example, is constructed of the radical for "body,"
尸 **shī** (*sheuh*), and 穴 **xuè** (*shreh*), meaning "hole" (which is
why so many people are uncomfortable writing the correct
character for this word—it just *looks* incredibly dirty).

Thanks to the modularity of Chinese, a word like **niúbī** can be thought of as being constructed of two building blocks ("cow" and "pussy") that can be taken apart and combined with other building blocks to make new (and often impressively logical) words. Thus on the "cow" side, we have words like:

Characters	Pinyin	Phonetic pronunciation	Literal translation	Meaning
牛肉	**niúròu**	*nyoo roe*	cow meat	beef
小牛	**xiǎoniú**	*shyow nyoo*	little cow	calf
牛排	**niúpái**	*nyoo pie*	cow ribs	steak
海牛	**hǎiniú**	*high nyoo*	sea cow	manatee
疯牛病	**fēngniúbìng**	*fuhng nyoo bing*	mad cow disease: 疯 **fēng** (*fuhng*) means "crazy," and 病 **bìng** (*bing*) means "sickness"	mad cow disease

And on the "pussy" side? This is where things get fun. For your convenience, below is a handy table—a cunt chart, if you will—of some of the many dirty words that use **bī**:

Characters	Pinyin	Phonetic pronunciation	Literal translation	Meaning
屄	**bī**	*bee*	pussy, cunt	pussy, cunt
牛屄	**niúbī**	*nyoo bee*	cow pussy	fuckin' awesome, badass, phat

傻屄	**shǎbī**	*shah bee*	idiot's pussy, stupid cunt	fuckin' idiot, motherfucker
大傻屄	**dà shǎbī**	*dah shah bee*	big dumb cunt	big fuckin' idiot, fuckin' motherfucker
装屄	**zhuāngbī**	*jwong bee*	**zhuāng** means "pretend" and the phrase implies the larger phrase **zhuāng niú bī**; that is, "pretending to be badass"	fuckin' poser
肏屄	**càobī**	*tsow bee*	fuck pussy	fuck, damn
妈屄	**mābī**	*mah bee*	mother's cunt	fuck, damn
肏你妈的屄	**cào nǐ mā de bī**	*tsow nee mah duh bee*	fuck your mother's cunt	fuck you
去你妈的屄	**qù nǐ mā de bī**	*chee nee mah duh bee*	go to your mother's pussy	fuck you; go to hell, motherfucker
你妈了个屄	**nǐmālagebī**	*nee mah lah guh bee*	your mother's a cunt	fuck you, what the fuck
老屄	**lǎobī**	*laow bee*	old cunt	old hag
骚屄	**sāobī**	*saow bee*	slutty cunt	slut, whore
屄毛	**bīmáo**	*bee maow*	pussy hair	pubic hair (vulgar)

CHAPTER TWO

The Chinese Art of Everyday Abuse

One of the first words you'll learn in Chinese class is 你好 **nǐhǎo** (*nee how*), which means "hello." However, the fact is that Chinese people don't actually say **nǐhǎo** all that often. Instead, when you arrive for dinner, a party, or a meeting, they'll say, "You've arrived," 你来了 **nǐ lái le** (*nee lie luh*). When you depart, someone will say, "You're going," 你走啦 **nǐ zǒu la** (*nee dzoe lah*).

When I walk down the street on a windy day, it seems the conversation is the same for everyone I pass. The granny taking her granddaughter out for a stroll will exclaim, as she lifts the little girl into her stroller, "It's windy!" The two middle-aged men running into each other on the street will greet each other by saying, "So windy today!" When I get home, the trash collector sitting on my stoop will welcome me back by announcing, "What a windy day!"

Chinese people love to comment on the obvious, sometimes to the point of insensitivity or what we might even consider outright cruelty. Chinese sports commentators often say things like "Wow, he's gained a lot of weight!" about athletes on the field. I have a "big-boned" older cousin whom, for as far back as I can remember, we have always called 胖姐姐 **pàng jiějie** (*pahng jyih jyih*), which literally means "fat sister." Westerners in China were once referred to as Big Nose. President Obama is often referred to as 黑人 **hēirén** (*hay ren*), or "the black guy." My bearded friend Jason is referred to as Big Beard. My mother is called the Mandarin equivalent of American Auntie, her older sister is Eldest Aunt, and my father is Old Man. It's as if every Chinese person is somehow living in gangland Chicago or some imaginary criminal underworld in which everyone needs a self-descriptive nickname to make it easier for the FBI to identify them. Indeed, the most notorious gang boss in Chinese history was "Big-Eared" Du, and his mentor was "Pockmarked" Huang.

And as if that wasn't bad enough, Chinese people, perhaps as a result of their collective thick skin, tend to demonstrate affection by being mean. Or rather, they speak frankly to each other in a way that, for them, indicates a level of familiarity that only a close relationship can have. But, to outside observers, it resembles, at best, a sort of constant, low-level stream of verbal abuse. For a young Chinese woman, there is no better way to express love for her boyfriend than by whacking him with her purse while telling him he's horrible. Groups of friends incessantly interrupt each other with cries of "Nonsense!" or "Shut up!" A good way to greet a pal is to give him a pained look and ask what the hell he did to his hair. I myself have had many an otherwise peaceful afternoon spent curled up on an armchair, happily reading a book, when I've been suddenly interrupted by a passing aunt or some other stray family member who snuck up behind me, smacked me across the back, and bellowed, "哎呀！又肥, 又蠢！" "**Āiyā! Yòu féi, yòu chǔn!**" (*aye yah! yo fay, yo chren!*): "My God! So fat and lazy!"

The Chinese word for "scold" or "verbally abuse" is 骂 **mà** (*mah*). Note those two squares at the top of the character—they represent two mouths, no doubt heaping abuse on the nearest person available. This chapter gathers words for the age-old art of 骂人 **màrén** (*mah ren*) or "scolding people," including everyday exclamations of annoyance and frustration, teasing put-downs and dismissals, words for affectionate name-calling, everyday insults, and everything else you'll need to generally convey to the most important people in your life that their very existence on this earth is a constant and overwhelming burden.

And finally, the Chinese may have a healthy sense of humor when it comes to the slings and arrows of everyday life, but they can also hold a grudge, and so at the end of the chapter you'll find words to fuel the fire when things cross the line into full-on feuding—genuinely venomous insults with the power to end decades-long friendships, provoke fistfights, and possibly get you disowned.

Everyday exclamations

哎呀 **àiya** (*aye yah*)

A common interjection that can be used for a wide range of occasions: when you've forgotten something, when you're impatient, when you're bored, when you feel helpless, as a lead-in to scolding someone, etc. It isn't exactly a word— more like a weighty sigh and roughly equivalent to "Oh Lord!" or "My God!"

糟了 **zāole** (*dzow luh*—the starting sound in *dzow* is like a buzzing *bzz* sound but with a *d* instead of a *b*, and the whole syllable should rhyme with "cow")

A very common expression of dismay. Literally "rotten" or "spoiled" and something like saying, "Oh shoot!" "Darn!" or "Crap!" You can also say 糟糕 **zāogāo** (*dzow gaow*—both syllables rhyme with "cow"), which literally means "rotten cakes," but it's less current.

完了 **wánle** (*wahn luh*)

Same meaning as **zāole** (above). It's pretty much like exclaiming "Crap!" to yourself. Literally, it means "over."

老天爷 **lǎotiānyé** (*laow tyinn yeh*)

Literally "my father God" and sometimes 我的天 **wǒdetiān** (*wuh duh tyinn*), literally "my heavens." Equivalent to exclaiming "My God!" or "Oh goodness!" These phrasings are more common among older people; younger people usually shorten them to 天哪 **tiānnǎ** (*tyinn nah*) or simply 天 **tiān** (*tyinn*): "Oh heavens!" or "Heavens!"

哇塞 **wā sài** (*wah sigh*)

Shoot! Darn! Oh my God! Wow! Holy cow! An exclamation especially popular among girls. Comes from a Taiwanese curse that means "Fuck your mother" (but is a shortened and nonprofane version of it).

该死的 **gāisǐde** (*guy sih duh*)

My God! Holy crap! Literally "should die."

气死我了 **qìsǐwǒle** (*chee sih wuh luh*)

Argh! Damn it! Crap! Literally, "I'm angry to the point of death."

可恶 **kěwù** (*kuh woo*)

Literally "hateful" and said alone means something like "Darn!"

傻眼 **shǎyǎn** (*shah yen*)

Oh no! Said in response to surprising, negative situations. For example, if you discover that your house has been broken into. Literally "dumbfounded eye."

晕 **yūn** (*een*)

Means "dizzy" or "faint" and is often uttered to express surprise, shock, amusement, or even confusion or disgust; that is, emotions that might make you feel faint.

倒霉 **dǎoméi** (*dow may*)

Bad luck. You can say this when something unfortunate happens. This sentiment can be made slightly stronger by saying 真倒霉 **zhēn dǎoméi** (*jen dow may*), which means "really bad luck."

点儿背 **diǎnr bēi** (*dyerr bay*)

Beijing/northern Chinese slang for **dǎoméi** (above), used the same way. Literally "fate turns its back on you." 点儿 **Diǎnr** is northern Chinese slang for "luck" or "fate," and 背 **bēi** means "back."

残念 **cánniàn** (*tsahn nyinn*)

Bummer, too bad. Popular among young people to express disappointment. Derived from the Japanese phrase *zannen desu*, which sounds similar and means something like "what a shame" or "that's too bad."

郁闷 **yùmēn** (*ee men*)

A popular term among young people, it means "depressed" but is used as an adjective for a much larger range of situations—when they feel pissed off, upset, disappointed, or even just bored. Exclaimed alone, one would say, "郁闷啊..." "**Yùmēn ā** ..." (*ee men ah*), meaning "I'm depressed ..." or "Sigh ..."

Dismissals and shutdowns

没劲 **méijìn** (*may jeen*)

Literally "no strength." Said dismissively of things you find uninteresting or stupid, much like saying "whatever." A stronger way to say this is 真没劲 **zhēn méijìn** (*jen may jeen*), literally "really no strength."

无聊 **wúliáo** (*ooh lyow*)

Nonsense, bored, boring. A common expression if you're bored is 无聊死了 **wúliáo sǐ le** (*ooh lyow sih luh*), literally "bored to death." You can also say **wúliáo** in response to something you find stupid or uninteresting; for example, in response to an unfunny joke.

服了 **fú le** (*foo luh*) or 服了你了 **fúle nǐ le** (*foo luh nee luh*)

Literally means "admire you" and sometimes said genuinely in response to something awe inspiring, but more usually said mockingly when someone says or does something silly or stupid. A more common form among younger people is "I 服了 U!" or "I **fú le** you," literally "I admire you," from a 1994 Stephen Chow movie.

不想耳食你 **bùxiǎngěrshíní** (*boo shahng er shih nee*)

I don't even want to talk to you; I'm ignoring you. Literally, "I don't want to ear eat you." Originally Sichuan slang.

帮帮忙 **bāngbāngmáng** (*bahng bahng mahng*)

Literally means "help" but used in Shanghai to admonish someone before rebutting something they've said. The equivalent of sarcastically saying "come on" or "please" or "give me a break."

小样了吧 **xiǎo yàng le ba** (*shyaow yahng luh bah*)

Said when laughing at or mocking someone else. Similar to "ha-ha" or "suck that." Used in northeastern China. Literally something like "(look at) that little face!"

哑了啊？ **yǎ le a?** (*yah luh ah*)

Literally, "Are you mute?" 哑 **Yǎ** means "dumb" or "mute." You can ask this when you say something and don't get a response.

歇菜 **xiē cài** (*shih tsigh*)

Knock it off; quit it. Literally "rest vegetable." A slangy but mild way to tell someone to stop doing something. Used in northern China only.

你吃错药了吗? **Nǐ chī cuò yào le ma?** (*nee chih tswuh yow luh ma*)

Did you take the wrong medicine? A mildly insulting way to imply that someone is acting rude or strange.

去! **Qù!** (*chee*)

Shut up! Literally "go." Usually said affectionately.

去你的! **Qù nǐ de!** (*chee nee duh*)

Get lost! Stop it! Up yours! Literally "go to yours."

闭嘴! **Bì zuǐ!** (*bee dzway*)

Shut up! Literally "close mouth." A more emphatic option is 你给我闭嘴! **Nǐ gěi wǒ bìzuǐ!** (*nee gay wuh bee dzway*), literally "Shut your mouth for me!"

切! **Qiè!** (*chyih*)

A noise expressing disdain. Equivalent to saying "Please!" or "Whatever."

烦 **fán** (*fahn*)

Irritating, annoying, troublesome. Common uses include 你烦不烦啊！ **Nǐ fán bù fán a!** (*nee fahn boo fahn ah*), meaning "You're really freaking annoying!" (literally, "Aren't you annoying!"), and 烦死人了你！ **Fánsǐ rén le nǐ!** (*fahn sih ren luh nee*): "You're annoying me to death!"

你恨機車 **nǐ hěn jīchē** (*nee hun gee chuh*)

You're really annoying. Taiwan slang for someone who is bossy or picky or otherwise annoying. Literally, "You are very motorcycle" or "You are very scooter." It's also common to just say 你恨機 **nǐ hěn jī** (*nee hun gee*) for short. Supposedly, this expression originally came from 雞歪 **jīwāi** (*gee why*), meaning one's dick is askew.

你二啊! **nǐ èr a!** (*nee er ah*)

You're so stupid. Literally, "You're [number] two." 二 **Er** (*er*) means "two" in Chinese, but in northeast China it can also be slang for "stupid" or "silly," referring to 二百五 **èrbǎiwǔ** (*er buy woo*) (see page 19).

脑子坏了吧？ **nǎozi huài le ba?** (*nee now dz hwie luh bah*)

Is your brain broken? Used exactly the way you'd use the English phrase.

你瞎呀? **nǐ xiā ya?** (*knee shah yah*)

Are you blind? Used, for example, when someone steps on your foot.

太过分了 **tài guòfèn le** (*tie gwuh fen luh*)

This is outrageous! This is going too far! Literally "much too far."

受不了 **shòubùliǎo** (*show boo lyaow*)

Literally "unacceptable" and can mean "This is unaccept-able" or "I can't take it." A stronger form is 真受不了 **zhēn shòubùliǎo** (*jen show boo lyaow*), literally "really unaccept-able."

你敢？ **nǐ gǎn?** (*nee gahn*)

Literally, "Do you dare?" and used in a challenging way when arguing or playing around. It's like saying, "Go ahead—I dare you!"

讨厌 **tǎoyàn** (*taow yen*—the first syllable rhymes with "cow")

Disgusting, troublesome, nuisance, nasty. Can also be a verb that means "to hate" (doing something). However, it is also common for girls to say this word by itself to express petu-lance, frustration, or annoyance.

你很坏! **nǐ hěn huài!** (*nee hun hwigh*)

You're so bad! Often used between friends in an unserious way or flirtingly between couples. However, like the rest of these expressions it can also be used in a genuinely angry way, perhaps by a mother toward a child. For example, 你怎么那么坏 **nǐ zěnme nàme huài** (*nee dzuh muh nuh muh hwigh*) means literally "How can you be so bad?" and is like saying, "*What* is wrong with you?"

恶心 **ěxīn** (*uhh sheen*)

Nauseating, disgusting, gross. Alternately, 真恶 **zhēn ě** (*jen uhh*), "very nauseating" or "so gross." **Ěxīn** can also be used as a verb to mean "to embarrass someone" or "to make someone feel uncomfortable or awkward."

没门儿 **méi ménr** (*may murr*)

No way! Fat chance! A rude, curt way to say no. Literally "no door." Used in Beijing.

废话 **fèihuà** (*fay hwa*)

Nonsense. Literally "useless words." An extremely common expression. Northern Chinese sometimes instead say 费! **fèi!** (*fay*), literally "wasteful," to mean "Nonsense!"

瞎说 **xiāshuō** (*shah shwuh*)

To talk nonsense. Literally "to speak blindly." Common usages include 别瞎说 **bié xiāshuō** (*byih shah shwuh*), meaning "don't be ridiculous" or "stop talking nonsense", and 你瞎说 **nǐ xiāshuō** (*nee shah shwuh*), "you're talking nonsense" or "you're full of crap."

Any of the following synonyms may be swapped for **xiāshuō** in the two samples given above:

> 胡扯 **húchě** (*hoo chuh*), "blab messily"
>
> 胡说 **húshuō** (*who shwuh*), "speak messily"
>
> 乱说 **luànshuō** (*lwun shwuh*), "speak chaotically"
>
> 鬼扯 **guǐchě** (*gway chuh*), "ghost blab"
>
> 说白话 **shuō báihuà** (*shwuh buy hwa*), "speak white words" (this one is seldom used among younger people now)

扯淡 **chědàn** (*chuh dahn*)

To talk nonsense, to bullshit (but not as profane as "bullshit"). Used in northern China.

放屁 **fàngpì** (*fahng pee*)

Bullshit, nonsense, lies, whatever, shut up! Literally "fart." Used as a mild expletive.

狗屁 **gǒupì** (*go pee*) or 放狗屁 **fàng gǒupì** (*fahng go pee*)

Bullshit, nonsense. Literally "dog fart" and "release a dog fart," respectively.

有屁快放 **yǒu pì kuaì fang** (*yo pee kwigh fahng*—**kuaì** rhymes with "high")

A more vulgar way to say "Spit it out!" or "If you have something to say, hurry up and say it." Literally means, "If you need to fart, hurry up and let it out."

屁话 **pìhuà** (*pee hwa*)

Bull, nonsense. Literally "fart talk." Can be exclaimed alone to mean "Nonsense!" or "Yeah, right!"

狗屁不通 **gǒupì bùtōng** (*go pee boo tohng*)

Incoherent, nonsensical. Literally "dog unable to fart." Exclaimed in response to something, it means roughly "that makes no sense" or "that's total bull." Can also be used as an adjective to describe someone who doesn't know what they're talking about.

(Mostly affectionate) name-calling

书呆子 **shūdāizi** (*shoo die dz*—**zi** sounds like saying a very short *bzz*, but with a *d* sound instead of the *b*)

Bookworm, nerd, lacking social skills. Literally "book idiot." 呆子 **Dāizi** means "idiot" or "fool" but is not often said alone.

懒虫 **lǎnchóng** (*lahn chong*)

Lazy bones. Literally "lazy bug." Said affectionately.

小兔崽子 **xiǎotù zǎizi** (*shaow too dzigh dz*—**zǎi** rhymes with "high")

Son of a rabbit. A gentle, teasing insult common among older people and directed at younger people. Ironically, parents often use this term to tease their children.

傻冒 / 傻帽 **shǎmào** (*shah maow*)

A gentle, affectionate jest—closer to something silly like "stupidhead." Literally "silly hat." 傻 **Shǎ** (*shah*) means "silly" or "dumb."

傻瓜 **shǎguā** (*shah gwah*)

Dummy, fool. Literally "silly melon." An extremely common insult, mostly used affectionately, and in use as early as the Yuan dynasty (1279—1368).

呆瓜 **dàiguā** (*die gwah*)

Dummy, fool. Literally "silly melon."

面 **miàn** (*myinn*)

Northern Chinese slang for "timid" or "weak." Literally "wheat flour," as in the ingredient for noodles and bread, suggesting that the person is soft and flimsy as those foods.

面瓜 **miànguā** (*myinn gwah*)

Timid, coward. Literally "timid melon" (or still more literally "flour melon"). Used only in northern China.

白痴 **báichī** (*buy chih*)

Perhaps the most universal and commonly used term for "idiot" or "moron."

十三点 **shísān diǎn** (*shh sahn dyinn*)

A mild, usually affectionate insult meaning "weirdo" or "crazy." Literally "thirteen o'clock." Originated in Shanghai and used a bit in other parts of southern China as well, though it is fast falling out of favor and is mainly used by older people now. The term refers to the **chī** in **báichī** (above), as the character for **chī**, 痴, is written using thirteen strokes. Other theories maintain that it refers to an illegal move in a gambling game called pai gow, 牌九 **páijiǔ** (*pie joe*) in Mandarin, or that it refers to an hour that clocks do not strike (though nowadays thirteen o' clock is possible in military time).

半弔子 / 半吊子 **bàn diàozi** (*bahn dyow dz*)

Someone deficient in skill or mental ability. In ancient China, copper coins had square holes in the center and were strung together on a string. One thousand coins strung together formed a **diào**. Half of that (five hundred coins) was called 半弔子 / 半吊子 **bàn diàozi** (*bahn dyow dz*). Northern Chinese only, and seldom used today, but necessary to understand the more commonly used insult below.

二百五 **èrbǎiwǔ** (*er buy woo*)

Dummy, idiot, moron. Literally "two hundred fifty," referring to half a **bàn diàozi** (see above). This is an extremely common insult; everyone knows it and probably grew up hearing it a lot, but like **shísān diǎn** (above), it's considered a bit old-fashioned now.

A number of (usually) affectionate Chinese insults involve eggs. They most likely come from the much stronger insult 王八蛋 **wángbādàn** (*wahng bah dun*), literally "son of a turtle" or "turtle's egg" and equivalent to "son of a bitch" or "bastard" in English. (The possible origins of **wángbādàn** are explained in the next chapter.) The insults below are mild and have shed any profane associations, much in the way we English speakers have mostly forgotten that phrases like "what a jerk," "that bites," and "sucker" originally referred to sex acts.

笨蛋 **bèndàn** (*ben dahn*)

Dummy, fool. Literally "stupid egg." 笨 **Bèn** (*ben*) alone can be used in many insults and means "stupid."

倒蛋 / 捣蛋 **dǎodàn** (*daow dahn*)

To cause trouble.

滚蛋 **gǔndàn** (*gwen dahn*)

Get lost! Literally "roll away, egg" or "go away, egg."

坏蛋 **huàidàn** (*hwigh dahn*)

Bad person. Literally "bad egg."

糊涂蛋 **hútúdàn** (*who too dahn*)

Confused/clueless person. Literally "confused egg."

穷光蛋 **qióngguāngdàn** (*chyohng gwahng dahn*)

An insulting term for a person without money. Literally "poor and have-nothing egg."

混蛋 **hùndàn** (*hwen dahn*)

Bastard. Literally "slacker egg." 混 **Hùn** (*hwen*) means "to loaf," "to wander around all day doing nothing," or "to be up to no good." Relatedly, 混混 **hùnhùn** (*hwen hwen*) or 混子 **hùnzǐ** (*hwen dz*) is used for a layabout, deadbeat, slacker, or any idle person up to no good.

龟孙子 **guī sūnzi** (*gway swen dz*) or 龟儿子 **guī érzi** (*gway er dz*)

Bastard. Literally "turtle grandson." An insult that has lost, like "egg" insults, any obscene connotation.

蠢货 **chǔnhuò** (*chwen hwuh*)

Dummy, moron. Literally "silly good."

菜 **cài** (*tsigh*)

Literally "vegetable." Can be an insulting term meaning "ugly" and may also be less insultingly used to describe someone who is bad at doing something. For example, 你电脑真菜 **nǐ diànnǎo zhēn cài** (*nee dyinn now jen tsigh*) means "You suck at using the computer." Similarly, 菜了 **cài le** (*tsigh luh*) is "to fail."

木 mù (*moo*)

Stupid, slow, insensitive. Literally "wooden."

脑子进水 nǎozi jìn shuǐ (*now dz jean shway*—zi is like saying a very short *bzz*, but with a *d* sound instead of the *b*)

Blockhead, dummy. Literally means "water in the brain."

脑子养鱼 nǎozi yǎng yú (*now dz yahng yee*)

Blockhead, dummy. Literally "fish feed in the brain" or "fish being raised in [one's] brain." A variant on "water in the brain" (above), more popular among younger people.

废人 fèirén (*fay ren*)

Useless person.

窝囊废 wōnangfèi (*wuh nahng fay*)

Loser. Literally "good-for-nothing useless."

软脚蟹 ruǎnjiǎoxiè (*rwun jow shih*)

Wuss, wussy, chicken. Literally "soft-legged crab." Originated in Suzhou, where crab legs are a popular food and strong legs with lots of meat are, obviously, preferred over soft legs with no meat. Mostly used in the South. Northerners do not use the term but do understand its meaning when they hear it.

吃素的 **chīsùde** (*chih soo duh*)

Wuss, pushover, sucker. Literally "vegetarian," referring to Buddhist monks because they are kind and merciful (and don't eat meat). Usually used defensively, as in 我可不是吃素的 **wǒ kě bushì chīsùde** (*wuh kuh boo shih chih soo duh*), "I'm not a wuss," or 你以为我是吃素的? **nǐ yǐwéi wǒ shì chīsùde?** (*nee ee way wuh shih chih soo duh*): "Do you think I'm a wuss?"

神经病 **shénjīngbìng** (*shen jing bing*)

Crazy, lunatic. Calling someone this connotes something like "What the hell is wrong with you?" Literally "mental illness."

有病 **yǒubìng** (*yo bing*)

Crazy. A slightly more common and mild variation on **shénjīngbìng** (above). It's like saying, "What? No way—you're crazy!" Literally "have a disease."

猪 **zhū** (*joo*) or 猪头 **zhūtóu** (*joo toe*)

Moron. Literally "pig" and "pighead," respectively.

半残废 **bàn cánfèi** (*bahn tsahn fay*)

Literally "half-handicapped" or "half cripple." Jokingly said of a man who is shorter than his woman. 残废 **Cánfèi** (*tsahn fay*) means "cripple" or "handicapped" and is a mocking term for a short man. Both terms can be real insults but, depending on who's saying them and how, can also be affectionate jests.

脑被驴踢了 **nǎo bèi lǘ tī le** (*now bay lee tee luh*)

Kicked in the head by a donkey. Popular among young people, used to call someone stupid.

痞子 **pǐzi** (*pee dz*)

A mild insult along the lines of "ruffian" or "riffraff." The literal meaning alludes to medical conditions of the liver, spleen, or abdomen, suggesting that **pǐzi** are like a disease on society.

没起子 **méi qǐzi** (*may chee dz*)

Useless, stupid, a good-for-nothing. Literally "no ambition."

弱智 **ruòzhì** (*rwuh jih*)

Idiotic, stupid. Literally "mentally enfeebled."

玩儿闹 **wánr nào** (*warr now*)

Troublemaker, ruffian. Also means "to fool around" or "to run wild." Beijing slang only. Literally "play and quarrel" or "play and loudly stir up."

冤大头 **yuān dàtóu** (*yren dah toe*)

Fool. Literally "wrong bighead."

浑球儿 **hún qíur** (*hwen chyurr*)

Good-for-nothing, rascal. Literally "unclear ball." 浑 **hun** means "unclear" or "dirty," as in 浑水 **hún shuǐ** (*hwen shway*), or "dirty water." Typically employed by parents to reprimand their kids. Used in northern China.

脑残 **nǎocán** (*now tsahn*)

Means "mental retardation" or "a mental disability" and is a popular insult among young people. One usage is 你脑残吗? **nǐ nǎocán ma?** (*nee now tsahn ma*), meaning "Are you retarded?" or "Is there something wrong with your head?"

脑有屎 **nǎo yǒu shǐ** (*now yo shih*) or 脑子里有屎 **nǎozi lǐ yǒu shǐ** (*now dz lee yo shih*)

Shit in the brain. Popular among young people.

The supernatural

瘟神 **wēn shén** (*when shen*)

A mild insult along the lines of "troublemaker." Literally "god of plague," referring to Chinese mythology. Considered old-fashioned now in much of China, but still used quite a bit in Sichuan Province and some southern areas.

鬼 **guǐ** (*gway*)

Means "devil" or "ghost." Not typically used as an insult in of itself, but often added onto adjectives to turn them into pejoratives. For example, if you think someone is selfish, or 小气 **xiǎo qì** (*shyaow chee*), you might call them a 小气鬼 **xiǎo qì guǐ** (*shyaow chee gway*), literally "selfish devil."

见鬼 **jiànguǐ** (*jyinn gway*)

Literally "see a ghost." Can be exclaimed alone to mean something like "Damn it!" or "Crap!" or "Oh shit!" But it is not profane like some of those English equivalents. Can also be used as an intensifier, as in 你见鬼去吧! **nǐ jiànguǐ qù ba!**

(*nee jinn gway chee bah*), which literally translates as "you see a ghost leave" but means "Go to hell!" or "Fuck off!" or "Get the hell out of my face!"

Rural insults

土 **tǔ** (*too*)

A pejorative with a broad range of meanings. It literally means "dirt" or "earth" and, most broadly, is used to describe an unsophisticated or uncultured person, much like "redneck" or "yokel" or "hick." Someone who spits on the floor while indoors, doesn't line up to buy things, or who can't figure out how to use the ticket-vending machine in the subway, might be called **tǔ**. **Tǔ** can also be a generic, somewhat all-purpose put-down, like "dork." More recently, **tǔ** refers to someone out of touch with aspects of modern society—for example, who doesn't know how to use the Internet.

土包子 **tǔ bāozi** (*too baow dz*)

Someone who is **tǔ**. (**Tǔ** is an adjective while **tǔ bāozi** is a noun.) One explanation for this term is that 包子 **bāozi** (a steamed, breadlike bun with meat or vegetable filling) is a common food in poor, rural areas, and so **tǔ bāozi** indicates that the person comes from the countryside.

老冒儿 **lǎo màor** (*laow murr*—the first syllable rhymes with "cow," and the second rhymes with "burr")

Northern Chinese slang for **tǔ**. Literally "old stupid" (though it can be said of anyone, not just old people). 冒 **Mào** is slang for "stupid" or "inexperienced" but is seldom used by itself anymore.

土得掉渣儿 **tǔ de diào zhār** (*to duh dyow jar*)

Ignorant, hick, unrefined. Literally "bumpkin shedding dirt," suggesting that someone is so **tǔ** that dirt is falling off them. Used in northeast China.

农民 **nóngmín** (*nohng meen*—**nóng** has a long *o* sound, like in "bone")

Literally means "farmer" or "peasant" (unlike in English, "peasant" is a neutral term in Chinese) but when said disdainfully can carry the same "country bumpkin" connotations as **tǔ** (above). However, **nóngmín** is not used nearly as often as **tǔ**.

柴禾妞儿 **chái he niūr** (*chai huh nyurr*)

An insulting term for a country girl, used in Beijing only.

没素质 **méi sùzhì** (*may soo jih*)

Literally "no quality." Said, like **tǔ**, of someone who acts in uncivilized ways and means he or she has no upbringing, manners, or class.

不讲文明 **bù jiǎng wénmíng** (*boo jyahng wen meeng*)

Same meaning as **méi sùzhì** (above) but less commonly used. Literally "not speaking civilization."

Extremely rude

烂人 **làn rén** (*lahn ren*)

Bad person. Literally "rotten person."

缩头乌龟 suō tóu wūguī (*swuh toe ooh gway*)

Coward. Literally "a turtle with its head in its shell."

臭 chòu (*choe*)

Stupid, bad, disappointing, inferior. Literally means "smelly" and is often added in front of insults to intensify them. So, for example, "smelly bitch" in Chinese, 臭婊子 **chòu biǎozi** (*choe byow dz*), is, as in English, much stronger than just "bitch."

丫头片子 yātóu piànzǐ (*yah toe pyinn dz*)

A Beijing insult for a young girl who's ignorant and inexperienced. 丫头 **Yātóu** means "servant girl." Literally "servant girl piece."

丑八怪 chǒubāguài (*choe bah gwie*)

An insulting term for an extremely ugly person. Literally "ugly all-around weird."

泼妇 pōfù (*pwuh foo*)

Shrew, bitch. An insulting term for a mean, crazy woman. Literally "spill woman."

三八 sānbā (*sahn bah*)

In Taiwan this just means "silly" and is said of both males and females, but on the mainland it is a very strong insult for a woman, similar to "bitch" or "slut." (Though sometimes it just means "gossipy.") Literally, it means "three eight," for which there are two explanations. One is that during the Qing dynasty (1644–1911) foreigners were supposedly only allowed to circulate on the eighth, eighteenth, and twenty-eighth of each month, and thus foreigners were called, somewhat scornfully, **sānbā** for the three eights. Another explanation is that **sānbā** refers to International Women's Day, which is on March 8. In contexts when it means "bitch" or "slut," it's common to amp up the strength of **sānbā** as an insult by saying 死三八 **sǐ sānbā** (*sih sahn bah*), literally "dead bitch," or 臭三八 **chòu sānbā** (*choe sahn bah*), literally "stinking bitch."

黄脸婆 **huángliǎnpó** (*hwahng lyinn pwuh*)

Slightly derogatory term for a middle-aged married woman. Literally "yellow-faced woman," meaning that she is old and ugly.

白眼狼 **báiyǎn láng** (*buy yen lahng*—the last syllable is similar to "long" but with an *ah* sound replacing the *o*)

Ingrate, a ruthless and treacherous person. Literally "white-eyed wolf." Both "white eyes" and "wolf" are insults in Chinese.

你不是人 **nǐ bú shì rén** (*nee boo shih ren*)

You're worthless; you're inhuman. Literally, "You are not a person."

你不是东西 **nǐ bú shì dōngxi** (*nee boo shih dohng she*)

You're worthless; you're less than human. Literally, "You're not a thing" or "You're not anything."

不要脸 **bùyàoliǎn** (*boo yaow lyinn*)

Shameless, without pride. Literally "doesn't want face." Face is a central concept in Chinese culture and entire volumes have been written in attempts to fully explain its nuances, but suffice to say that losing face is bad, giving face is good, and not wanting face is unspeakably shameful—thus saying that someone is **bùyàoliǎn** is far more insulting than the English word "shameless" and conveys a complex mix of being somehow subhuman, pathetic, and so lacking in self-respect that you would willingly do things that no one else would be caught dead doing. Also used by women to mean "disgusting" and sometimes with 臭 **chòu** (*cho*, rhymes with "show"), which means "stinking," in front to amplify it to 臭不要脸 **chòu bùyào liǎn**, or "absolutely disgusting." Another common way to amplify the expression is to say 死不要脸 **sǐ bù yào liǎn** (*sih boo yow lyinn*), literally, "You don't want face even when you die."

去死 **qù sǐ** (*chee sih*)

Go die.

走狗 **zǒugǒu** (*dzoe go*—both syllables rhyme with "oh")

Lackey, sycophant. Literally "running dog." Said of a servile person with no morals who sucks up to more powerful people.

狗腿子 **gǒutuǐzi** (*go tway dzz*) / 狗腿 **gǒutuǐ** (*go tway*)

A variant of **zǒugǒu** (above). Literally "dog legs." You may have heard of the term "capitalist running dog" or "imperialist running dog." Mao Zedong used "dog legs" to refer to countries that were friendly with the United States.

滚 **gǔn** (*gwen*) or 滚开 **gǔnkāi** (*gwen kigh*) or 滚蛋 **gǔndàn** (*gwen dun*)

Go away; get lost.

老不死的 **lǎo bù sǐ de** (*laow boo sih duh*)

A rude term for an old person. Literally "old and not dead."

老东西 **lǎo dōngxi** (*laow dohng she*)

Old thing. A rude term for an old person.

老模砢磣眼 **lǎo mó kē chěn yǎn** (*laow mwuh kuh chen yen*)

Literally "old wrinkle eyes." An insulting term for someone old and ugly. Used in Beijing.

垃圾 **lājī** (*lah gee*)

Literally "trash" but can be derogatorily said of people as well. In Taiwan pronounced **lè se** (*luh suh*).

畜生 **chùshēng** (*choo shung*)

Animal, inhuman. Literally "born of an animal." An extremely strong insult.

Slut and whore

In addition to the terms below, chapter 7, "Behaving Badly," includes numerous words for "prostitute" that can also be used as strong insults.

骚货 **sāohuò** (*saow hwuh—***sāo** rhymes with "cow")

Slut (but can also be said of a man). Literally "lewd thing."

贱货 **jiànhuò** (*gin hwuh*)

Slut (but can also be said of a man). Literally "cheap thing."

婊子 **biǎozi** (*byow dz*)

Can literally mean "whore" but also used as a strong insult for a woman, equivalent to "bitch" or "whore." Often strengthened to 臭婊子 **chòu biǎozi** (*choe byow dz*), literally "stinking whore."

狐狸精 **húlijīng** (*hoo lee jing*)

Vixen, tart, slut. A woman who seduces other people's husbands or boyfriends. Literally "fox-spirit," referring to a creature from Chinese mythology. Slightly milder than the other terms for "slut."

风骚 **fēngsāo** (*fung sow*, the latter rhymes with "cow")

Slutty. Literally "sexy and horny."

公共汽车 **gōnggòngqìchē** (*gohng gohng chee chuh*—the first two syllables sound like "gong" but with a long *o*, or *oh*, sound in the middle)

Slut, a woman who sleeps around. Literally "public bus," as in "everyone has had a ride." Similar to the English expression "the neighborhood bicycle."

荡妇 **dàngfù** (*dahng foo*)

Slut. Literally "lustful woman."

残花败柳 **cán huā bài liǔ** (*tsahn hwah buy lew*—**liǔ** rhymes with "pew")

An insult meaning "old whore." Literally "broken flower, lost willow." Used mostly in northern China.

CHAPTER THREE

Swearing and Profanity

In English, we have plenty of ways to curse, but for the most part we tend to rely on a small and rather unvaried stable of fallback words. Similarly, the Chinese language allows you to spin an infinite number of creative, colorful curses, but you're much more likely to stick with a basic like "fuck you."

As in English, most Chinese swearing centers on fucking and its related accoutrements (the pussy and penis). And lots of insults involve stupidity or illegitimate birth or prostitution—nearly direct equivalents to "stupid cunt," "fucking bastard," "dirty whore," "what a dick," etc.

There are, however, a few major differences between the two languages. For one thing, China is officially an atheist country, so there is no real equivalent to Christian (or Muslim) blasphemy—nothing mirroring "Holy God!" or "Jesus Christ!" or "Damn you to hell!" Several terms in this chapter are translated as "damn" but really to indicate in English how strong—or in this context *not* strong—of an obscenity the word is. The concepts of heaven, hell, and devils, however, do exist in China, stemming from Buddhist and Taoist traditions, and thus you can call someone a devil, tell someone to go to hell, and launch a few other insults along those lines, but they are not very common and are considered old-fashioned and mild (the few examples of such insults worth mentioning appear in the previous chapter). Perhaps the closest thing to religious blasphemy in Chinese is the cursing of one's ancestors, which is a serious insult as Chinese culture places a great deal of importance on blood ties, and ancestor worship is still practiced in some of the more traditional parts of the country.

Another way in which Chinese differs from English is that words relating to homosexuality (see chapter 6) are not particularly used as insults. This, again, may have something to do with the lack of religious dogma in China. While homosexuality is not exactly accepted in Chinese society, being gay does not carry the stigma of inherent moral "wrongness" that it often bears in Christian and Muslim societies. (Homosexuality can be considered bad in China for plenty of other reasons, but they mostly have to do with the importance that society places on having children.) Thus there is nothing in the Chinese vocabulary like "cocksucker," "faggot," "bugger off," "that's so gay," or "that sucks."

One final mainstay of English-language swearing conspicuously absent from Chinese is "shit." In a country that until recently was predominantly agricultural (meaning that manure was an important resource), where people talk openly at the dinner table about diarrhea, and where babies toddle about with their naked butts exposed in "split pants" (pants open at the back so that Junior can squat wherever he wants and take an impromptu dump on the street), it just isn't very dirty to mention excrement or urine.

This is not to imply, however, that shit is entirely neutral in Chinese. Any mention of shit is vulgar, and thus certainly not fit for, say, the classroom or the office; it just isn't used as an actual swear word like it is in English. You might use it when you're purposely being gross, such as while joking around with family or good friends. But in those cases talking about shit would be just crude enough to be funny but not outright dirty. And as with any vulgar word, "shit" can also be used in an insulting way. One might say, for example, "That movie sucked so hard it made me want to shit," or "The team played like shit." For that reason, this chapter includes a few pejorative words and phrases involving shit, but you'd use them more to be bawdy than to actually swear. In fact, the very idea of using "shit" pejoratively is probably a Western import that was popularized through the subtitling of Western movies in Hong Kong.

The words and phrases in this chapter will give you all the vocabulary necessary to hold your own with even the most salty-tongued of Chinese. Many of these words can be used affectionately with close friends—in the way you might call a buddy "motherfucker" in English—but don't forget that, no matter how close you think you are to someone, doing so can be hard to pull off when you don't quite grasp all the nuances of the dialogue. And another note of caution on using strong language in Chinese: if you are a woman, using these words will, in some situations, cause outright shock. Chinese society right now is a bit like America in the fifties— there are certain things a girl just isn't supposed to do. Feel free to let your verbosity run wild in the appropriate contexts (the proximity of chain-smoking, booze-swilling, young Chinese women should be a helpful clue). And of course there are times when shock might be the exact effect you're going for (like, say, when some asshole tries to scam you on the street). But for the most part, in the eyes of most Chinese, any word that appears in this chapter is (along with the stronger insults from the previous chapter) something that should never escape a lady's mouth.

Fuck-related profanity

肏 **cào**, more commonly written 操 **cāo** (both pronounced *tsow*)

Fuck. The character 肏 is visually quite graphic, as it is composed of 入 **rù** (*roo*), meaning "enter," and 肉 **ròu** (*row*), meaning "meat." 肏 is technically the correct character for "fuck," but because it is not included in most computer or phone-character input systems, and because it's just so uncomfortably dirty looking, most people write the homophonous 操 (which actually means "hold"). Thus I have written 操 for the rest of the terms in this chapter that use the word. But remember, technically, it should be 肏. (For those of you who pay attention to pinyin tones, I also render the syllable as fourth tone every time even though 操 is first tone, since that's pretty much how it always comes out sounding. In general, though, with colloquial expressions like these you shouldn't get too hung up on which tone is technically accurate since it's not always fixed.)

我操 **wǒ cào** (*wuh tsow*)

Fuck! An extremely common exclamation for all occasions—when you're pissed off, impressed, amazed, or whatever. Literally, "I fuck." (As a side note, many Chinese are amused when they hear English speakers say "what's up?" or "wassup?" because it sounds to them like **wǒ cào**.) When saying "fuck" alone, it's much more usual to say **wǒ cào** than to say just 操 **cào** (*tsow*); northern Chinese, however, do often use **cào** alone as an interjection, especially between clauses. For example: "I had a really bad morning, fuck, had a car accident on my way to work."

操你妈 **cào nǐ mā** (*tsow nee ma*)

Fuck you! Literally, "Fuck your mother!" An extremely common obscenity.

操你大爷 **cào nǐ dàye** (*tsow nee dah yeh*)

Fuck you! Literally, "Fuck your grandfather!" Northern and southern Chinese use different words for grandparents, so this one is used in northern China only. This is marginally less strong than **cào nǐ mā** (above) because it's generally considered more offensive to curse someone's female relatives than their male relatives. You can insert any relative into this construction; for example northern Chinese might say 操你奶奶 **cào nǐ nǎinai** (*tsow nee nigh nigh*): literally, "Fuck your grandmother." See the entries after 日 **rì** (page 39) for the southern versions.

操你妈的屄 **cào nǐ mā de bī** (*tsow nee ma duh bee*)

Fuck you! Literally, "Fuck your mother's cunt," and stronger than the two expressions above since you're adding another obscene word, **bī**, or "pussy," on top of **cào**.

操屄 **càobī** (*tsow bee*)

Fuck. Can be exclaimed alone or used as an intensifier. Literally, "fuck pussy."

操蛋 **càodàn** (*tsow dahn*)

Literally "fuck egg." (See the previous chapter for why eggs are used in insults.) Can be exclaimed alone, like "Fuck!" or "Oh fuck!" and can also be used as an adjective to mean that someone is bad or inept, as in 你真肏蛋 **nǐ zhēn càodàn** (*nee jen tsow dahn*), which means "You're a real stupid fuck."

操行 **càoxing** (*tsow sheeng*)

A dirty and insulting way to refer to someone's appearance or behavior. Literally "fucking behavior" or something like "the behavior of a shitty person." For example, 你看他那操行, 真受不了 **nǐ kàn tā nà càoxíng, zhēn shòubùliao** (*nee kahn tah tsow sheeng, jen show boo liao*) means "Look at his shit behavior, it's totally unacceptable." The term can also be an adjective meaning "shameful" or "disgusting," as in 你真操行 **nǐ zhēn càoxíng** (*nee jen tsow sheeng*), or "You're really fucking disgusting."

操你八辈子祖宗! **Cào nǐ bā bèizi zǔzōng!** (*wuh tsow nee bah bay dz dzoo dzohng*)

Fuck eight generations of your ancestors! An extremely strong insult: stronger than **cào nǐ mā** (above). It's always specifically eight or eighteen generations that are cursed in this insult. The number eight, 八 **bā** (*bah*), is considered lucky in Chinese culture. Thus it is especially significant for misfortune to befall what should be a lucky number of generations.

操你祖宗十八代! **Cào nǐ zǔzōng shíbā dài!** (*tsow nee dzoo dzohng shih bah die*)

Fuck eighteen generations of your ancestors! An extremely strong insult. All multiples of nine are significant in Chinese

culture because nine, 九 **jiǔ** (*joe*), is pronounced the same as the word for "long-lasting," written 久. Eighteen, 十八 **shíbā** (*shih bah*), is itself significant because it sounds like 要发 **yào fā** (*yow fah*), which means "one will prosper."

日 **rì** (*rih*)

Southern Chinese slang for "fuck" (and also used a bit in some northern provinces like Shanxi and Shandong.) Its origins most likely come from it sounding like 入 **rù** (*roo*), which means "enter" and in ancient China was itself a less dirty way of saying "fuck" (like saying "freaking" instead of "fucking"). **Rù** is also a component radical for another word for "fuck," 入 **cào** (see page 36). **Rì** is used the same way as **cào**—combined with "I" into an exclamation like 我日! **Wǒ rì!** (*wuh rih*), meaning "Fuck!" or directed at someone's mother or relatives or ancestors to mean "Fuck you!" as in 日你妈! **Rì nǐ mā!** (*rih nee ma*), literally, "Fuck your mother!"

日你外公 **rì nǐ wàigōng** (*rih nee why gohng*)

Fuck you. Literally, "Fuck your grandfather!" Used in southern China.

日你外婆 **rì nǐ wàipó** (*rih nee why pwuh*)

Fuck you. Literally, "Fuck your grandmother!" Used in southern China.

干 **gān** (*gahn*)

Fuck. In reality, **gān** is slightly less offensive than **cào** (see above), partly because it isn't visually graphic (like 肏). It's closer in strength to "shit," but most dictionaries translate it as "fuck." It can refer to having sex, and the way it's used grammatically is also closer to "fuck"—it can be yelled alone when you're pissed off, as in 干! **Gān!** (*gahn*) or 干了! **Gānle!** (*gahn luh*), or like **cào** it can followed by a subject (usually someone's mother). See the next entry for more on this. Also see chapter 5 for how to use **gān** in the context of describing sex. The character 干 also means "dry," which has made for more than a few comical mistranslations on Chinese restaurant menus and supermarket signs. Now you'll know what happened next time you come across "sliced fuck tofu" on a Chinese menu. 干 **Gān** is also used a lot in fighting contexts because it can also mean "to kill."

干你娘 **gān nǐ niáng** (*gahn nee nyahng*)

Fuck you! Literally, "Fuck your mother!" Used in southern China only (a northerner would always say **cào nǐ mā**). 娘

Niáng means "mother," same as 妈 **mā** (*ma*), but 干你妈 **gān
nǐ mā** sounds funny in Chinese so **niáng** is always used instead.

靠 kào (*cow*)

Damn! A common exclamation to express surprise or anger.
靠 **Kào** means "to depend upon" in Mandarin, but in the
southern Fujianese dialect that the expression originates
from (spoken in both Fujian and Taiwan) it's actually 哭 **kū**
(*coo*), meaning "to cry." **Kao bei,** "cry over your father's
death," **kao bu,** "cry over your mother's death," and **kao yao,**
"cry from hunger," are extremely common expressions (implying something like "What's wrong with you? Did your
mother/father just die?" or "Are you dying of starvation?")
and are nasty ways, in this dialect, to tell someone to shut
up. However, in its popularization beyond Fujian and Taiwan the meaning has changed to an exclamation equivalent
to "Damn!"

我靠 wǒ kào (*wuh cow*)

Shit! A common exclamation to express surprise or anger. In
Mandarin, it literally means "I depend on" but is used as a
stronger form of **kào,** like "Shit!" versus "Damn!"

Cursing mothers (and other relatives)

他妈的 tāmāde (*tah mah duh*)

Damn! Shit! While not anywhere near as vulgar as the words
above, this is without a doubt the most classic of Chinese
swears. It means "his mother's" and implies the larger sentence 操他妈的屄 **cào tā mā de bī** (*tsow tah mah duh bee*),
"Fuck his mother's pussy!" but is much less dirty since the

key words are left out. The phrase can be exclaimed by itself or used to intensify an adjective. Thus you can say something like "今天他妈的冷" **"Jīntiān tāmāde leng"** (*jean tyinn tah mah duh lung*) for "Today is really damn cold," even though the literal translation, "Today is his mother's cold," doesn't make sense. Another example: 他真他妈的牛屄! **Tā zhēn tāmāde niúbī!** (*tah jen tah ma duh nyoo bee*) means "He's really fucking badass!" even though it translates as "He's really his mother's awesome!"

And of course, you can swap in any other relatives—a common version in Beijing is 他大爷 **tā dàye** (*tah dah yeh*), literally "his grandfather" (implying "his grandfather's"). 他奶奶的 **Tā nǎinai** (*tah nigh nigh*), "his grandmother" (implying "his grandmother's") is common as well.

你老师 **nǐ lǎoshī** (*nee laow shih*)

Damn! Literally "your teacher" (implying "his teacher's"). A Taiwan variation on **tāmāde** (page 41). Written 你老師 in Taiwan.

妈的 **māde** (*mah duh*)

Damn! Literally "mother's" and a shortened form of **tāmāde** (page 41). Both an exclamation and an intensifier.

你妈的 **nǐmāde** (*nee mah duh*)

Damn you! Literally "your mother's" instead of "his mother's" (page 41) and thus a bit stronger since it's a direct address.

你大爷 **nǐ dàye** (*nee dah yeh*)

Damn you! A northern Chinese variation on the above. Literally "your grandfather" (implying "your grandfather's").

你奶奶 **Nǐ nǎinai** (*nee nigh nigh*), "your grandmother," is common in northern China as well.

他大爷 **tā dàye** (*tah dah yeh*)

Shit, damn. Can be either exclaimed alone or used as an intensifier. Literally "his grandfather." 他奶奶 **Tā nǎinai** (*tah nigh nigh*), "his grandmother," is common as well. Both are only used in northern China.

去你妈的 **qù nǐ mā de** (*chee nee mah duh*)

Fuck off. Literally "go to your mother's" and stronger than **tāmāde** (page 41) since it is a direct address.

去你奶奶的 **qù nǐ nǎinai de** (*chee nee nigh nigh duh*)

Fuck off. Literally "go to your grandmother's" and a variation on the above.

去你的 **qùnǐde** (*chee nee duh*)

Damn you, get lost. Literally "go to yours" and milder than the above.

你妈的屄 **nǐ mā de bī** (*nee ma duh bee*)

Fuck! Fuck you! Can be exclaimed alone or addressed at someone. Literally "your mother's cunt."

叫你生孩子没屁股眼 **jiào nǐ shēng háizi méi pìguyǎn** (*jaow nee shung hi dz may pee goo yen*)

Literally, "May your child be born without an asshole." A very strong curse. Sometimes 没屁股眼 **méi pìguyǎn** (*may pee goo yen*) by itself ("no asshole," or more technically "imperforate anus") is used as a curse like "Damn!" Originated in

Hong Kong and surrounding southern areas, but now commonly used all over China.

Cunt-related obscenities

牛屄 **niúbī** (*nyoo bee*)

Can be used negatively to mean something like "arrogant fuck" but more usually means "fuckin' awesome" or "motherfuckin' badass." Think of it as meaning that someone has a lot of fuckin' balls, either in a good way or a bad way. Literally "cow pussy" (see chapter 1 for the etymology). Extremely popular in northern China, where it originated, and not as commonly used but still understood in southern China. Not used at all (and will most likely not be understood) in Taiwan.

傻屄 shǎbī (*shah bee*)

Stupid cunt, fuckin' idiot. Literally "idiot's pussy"—傻 **shǎ** (*shah*) means "stupid." Particularly in northern China, this is perhaps *the* strongest, dirtiest insult available in your arsenal of things to yell at that fucker who just cut you off in traffic or who just tried to mug you on the street. It also sounds a lot like "shabby," as many English teachers in China have unwittingly discovered when attempts to teach the word are met with peals of laughter. Like **niúbī**, it is extremely common in northern China, less used in southern China, and not used at all in Taiwan.

装屄 zhuāngbī (*jwong bee*)

Act like a fuckin' poser; be a fuckin' ass. Literally "dress pussy" or "pretend pussy." 装 **Zhuāng** (*jwong*) means "pretend" or "put on," like putting on an item of clothing, and implies the larger phrase 装牛屄 **zhuāng niúbī** (*jwong nyoo bee*); that is, pretending to be **niúbī**, or awesome, when you're not. Thus you could say that you don't like going to fancy restaurants because you don't want to be surrounded by all those **zhuāngbī** types. Again, extremely common in northern China, less used in southern China, and not used at all in Taiwan.

二屄 (more usually written 二逼 or 2B) èrbī (*er bee*)

Fuckin' idiot, a fuck-up. Used in northern China. Literally "second pussy" or "double cunt." 二 **Ér**, or "two," is a reference to the insult "250," or 二百五 **èrbǎiwǔ** (*er buy woo*), which means "idiot" (see page 19).

臭屄 chòubī (*choe bee*)

Motherfucker. Literally "smelly cunt" or "stinking cunt."

烂屄 **lànbī** (*lahn bee*)

Rotten cunt.

妈屄 **mābī** (*mah bee*)

Hag, cunt. Literally "mother's cunt."

老屄 **lǎobī** (*laow bee*)

Old cunt, old hag.

骚屄 **sāobī** (*saow bee*)

Slut, dirty cunt. Literally "slutty cunt." A stronger, or at least slightly more colorful, variation on plain 屄 **bī** (*bee*).

屄样 **bīyàng** (*bee yahng*)

Literally "the appearance of a cunt," referring to someone's behavior in a way that indicates that they're being a cunt, or you think they're a cunt. Similar to **càoxing**, discussed earlier in this chapter.

鸡屄 **jībī** (*gee bee*)

鸡 **jī** (*gee*), literally "chicken," or 鸡贼 **jī zéi** (*gee dzay*), literally "chicken thief," is Beijing slang for someone cheap or stingy, and 鸡屄 **jībī**, literally "chicken cunt," is a dirty version of that term.

你妈了个屄 **nǐmālegebī** (*nee mah luh guh bee*)

Fuck you! (and a way of saying it that rolls off the tongue especially well). Literally, "Your mother's a cunt!"

你个死屄 **nǐ ge sǐ bī** (*nee guh sih bee*)

Literally "you dead cunt," but the whole phrase can be used the way you'd use "fuck" in direct address, whether genuinely insulting someone or joking around, like "fuck you" or "you stupid fuck."

Dick-related swears

屌 **diǎo** (*dyaow*)

Slang for "cock" and used as an insult (as in "what a dick") since the Jīn dynasty (1115–1234). **Diǎo** is also used positively in Taiwan to mean "awesome" or "cool" or "outrageous."

管你屌事 **guǎn nǐ diǎo shì** (*gwun nee dyow shih*)

Mind your own damn business. Literally "mind your own dick." Similarly, "It's none of my damn business" or "I don't give a shit" is 管我屌事 **guǎn wǒ diǎo shì** (*gwun wuh dyow shih*), literally, "I'm watching my own dick."

鸟 **niǎo** (*nyow*, rhymes with "cow")

Slang for "penis," equivalent to "dick" or "cock," but can also be combined with a noun to create a derogatory term; for example 那个人 **nàge rén** (*nah guh ren*) means "that person," while 那个鸟人 **nàge niǎo rén** (*nyow ren*) means "that dick" or "that damned person."

什么鸟 **shénmeniǎo** (*shuh muh nyow*)

Used similarly to "what the fuck?" or "what in the hell?" Literally "which bird?" or "what dick?" Originated in northeastern China but now used everywhere.

鸡巴 **jība** (*gee bah*)

Slang for "penis," equivalent to "dick" or "cock." Like "dick" and "cock," **jība** can refer to an actual penis or can be used as an insult to describe a person. It's also used as an intensifier, like "fucking." For example, 那个鸡巴白痴 **nàge jībā báichī** (*nah guh gee bah buy chih*), "that fucking idiot," is stronger than 那个白痴 **nàge báichī** (*nah guh buy chih*), "that idiot."

Turtle swears

There are several turtle- and turtle-egg-related insults in Chinese, all connected to cuckoldry. There are numerous theories why. One is that 王八蛋 **wángbādàn** (*wahng bah dun*), "tortoise egg," comes from 忘八端 **wàng bā duān** (*wahng bah dwun*), which means "forgetting the Eight Virtues," because the two phrases sound nearly identical. The Eight Virtues are a philosophical concept and a sort of code of behavior central to Confucianism. Evidently the Eight Virtues were important enough that forgetting them could become an obscenity, much in the way Christianity is so central to Western culture that referring to God—"Oh my God!" "Jesus Christ!"—can be considered blasphemous.

Another theory—and all these theories could be related to one another—is that the ancient Chinese mistakenly believed there were no male turtles and that all turtles copulated with snakes; thus their offspring are of impure blood. Another explanation is that in ancient times 王八 **wángbā** (*wahng bah*), "turtle," was the name for a male servant in a brothel. Some believe the term came from an especially unvirtuous man in history whose last name was Wáng (王). Still another is that a turtle's head emerging from its shell resembles a glans penis emerging from the foreskin and so turtles represent promiscuity: indeed "glans" in Chinese is

龟头 **guītóu** (*gway toe*), or "turtle head." And finally, it could have to do with turtles being considered cowardly, since they sink their heads back into their shells when threatened, as reflected by the phrase 缩头乌龟 **suō tóu wūguī** (*swuh toe ooh gway*), "a turtle with its head in its shell," meaning "coward."

王八 **wángbā** (*wahng bah*)

Cuckold, bastard, asshole, piece of shit.

王八蛋 **wángbādàn** (*wahng bah dun*)

Son of a bitch, bastard. Literally "tortoise egg."

王八羔子 **wángbā gāozi** (*wahng bah gaow dz*)

Son of a bitch, bastard. Literally "son of a turtle" and a northern variation on **wáng bā dàn**.

王八犊子 **wángba dúzi** (*wahng bah doo dz*)

Son of a bitch, bastard. Literally "turtle stomach," probably alluding to the pregnant belly of a cuckold's wife, suggesting, like **wángbādàn**, "turtle's egg," that the target of the insult doesn't know who his father is.

龟儿子 **guī ér zi** (*gway er dz*)

Son of a bitch, bastard. Literally "son of a turtle." A variation on **wángbādàn** used only in southern China.

龟孙子 **guī sūnzi** (*gway swen dz*)

Son of a bitch, bastard. Literally "turtle's grandson." Another variation on **wángbādàn** used only in southern China.

Dog-related swears and insults

狗崽子 / 狗仔子 **gǒuzǎizi** (*go dzigh dzz*)

Son of a bitch (although a bit milder than the English). Literally "son of a dog."

狗娘养的 **gǒu niáng yǎng de** (*go nyahng yahng duh*)

Son of a bitch (rude—more so than the previous entry). Literally, can mean "raised by a dog mother" or "born of a dog mother."

狗日的 **gǒurìde** (*go rih duh*)

Son of a bitch (rude). Literally, can mean "fucked by a dog" or "born of a mother fucked by a dog."

狗杂种 **gǒu zázhǒng** (*go dzah dzohng*)

Literally "mongrel dog," a variation on 杂种 **zázhǒng** (*dzah dzohng*), another insult meaning "mixed blood." Extremely rude.

Shit

屎 **shǐ** (*shih*)

Shit (noun), like shit (adverb), shitty (adjective). You would use this to describe things. For example, you might say 太屎了 **tài shǐ le** (*tie shih luh*), literally "too shitty," to say that something was shitty or bad. Sometimes written "10" online because both are pronounced *shih*.

狗屎 **gǒushǐ** (*go shih*)

Bullshit. Literally "dog shit." This term was originally used to describe people of low moral character. This new usage is probably due to Western influence—it started out in Hong Kong and Taiwan, where "Oh shit!" in Hollywood movies was often subtitled **gǒushǐ**, and spread from there.

臭狗屎 **chòu gǒushǐ** (*choe go shih*)

Stronger form of above. Literally "smelly dog crap."

屎盆子 **shǐ pénzǐ** (*shih pen dz*)

Shitty job, the blame for doing a shitty job. Literally "crap pot." You might say, for example, that someone gave you the crap pot, meaning that they made you take the blame for a shitty job. Or you can describe something directly as a crap pot, meaning that it was done poorly.

吃屎 **chī shǐ** (*chih shih*)

Eat shit. Equivalent to "fuck off," though much less profane.

粪 **fèn** (*fen*)

Feces (formal term). You wouldn't say this alone as an adjective, like "shitty," but one common Beijing expression is 臭大粪 **chòu dà fèn** (*choe dah fen*), literally "stinky big stool," meaning that something is shitty or worthless.

大便 **dàbiàn** (*dah byinn*)

Excrement, poop, defecate (both noun and verb). Literally "big relieving of oneself"—urination, by the way, is 小便 **xiǎobiàn** (*dah byinn*), "small relieving of oneself." Not an expletive, and thus does not have the same effect as "shit." For the most part, this refers to the actual act of defecation and its product, but can be used mockingly, in a silly and unserious way, like calling someone a poop. Girls in particular use this teasingly.

去吃大便 **qù chī dàbiàn** (*chee chih dah byinn*)

Go eat excrement; go eat poop. Similar to saying "get lost." Sounds mild and silly, so it's mostly used by girls in a teasing way.

Writing

傻 X **shǎchā** (*shah chah*)

This is often used in written Chinese to stand in for a dirty word. Literally "stupid X." X is pronounced *chah* in Chinese.

CHAPTER FOUR

Men and Women: Flirting, Dating, Love, and Marriage

It's hard to be in China for long without noticing the prevalence of not terribly attractive Western men who seem to have inexplicably landed themselves a gorgeous Chinese girlfriend. Though I hesitate to offer any explanation for this phenomenon, I do find myself recalling an awful lot of conversations with Chinese gal-pals about their inability to tell westerners apart. I may or may not have told some of these women to be sure and introduce me to any prospective beaus before taking the plunge, so that I could distinguish for them the handsome men from the mugs that even a mother wouldn't love.

Then again, maybe these women know exactly what they've gotten themselves into, as more than a few pragmatically minded Chinese women have counseled me on the importance of choosing someone "bald and fat"—the reasoning being that such mates will be less likely to cheat or leave you. And on top of all that, you never know what

seemingly smoking hot girl is considered downright homely by Chinese beauty standards. I have pointed out plenty of what I thought to be beautiful women, only to have Chinese friends reply musingly, "Yes, it's strange, my other Western friends think she's hot too. We all think she looks like a peasant."

But perhaps we should just be glad that cross-cultural blindness is enabling people everywhere to get laid. In this chapter, you'll find all the vocabulary you need for flattering, cajoling, and hopefully landing a date—or more. But read with caution: dating in China is a whole new ball game. The essential thing to know is this: the woman wears the pants in the relationship. Though we certainly can't stereotype every Chinese woman this way, should you as a Western male choose to embark upon a relationship with one, be prepared to pay for everything (possibly including her rent), call and text her ten times a day (being tied up in meetings at work all day is no excuse), secure her permission whenever you want to go out with the guys (it will not be granted), and always, always, carry her purse (no matter how shiny, pink, or Hello Kitty bedecked it may be). And should you Western women desire to learn the ways of Chinese dating, you'd better brush up on the art of 撒娇 **sǎjiāo** (*sah jow*)—a common, whiney way of acting that most westerners find maddening and Chinese presumably find cute—which essentially involves pouting a lot, speaking in the voice of a five-year-old, hitting your boyfriend a lot whilst calling him "so bad," and, of course, making him carry your purse.

Finding Love

调情 **tiáoqíng** (*tyow cheeng*)

To flirt. Literally "throw feelings."

挑逗 **tiǎodòu** (*tyow doe*)

To flirt. Literally "incite and tease."

打情骂俏 **dǎ qíng mà qiào** (*dah ching ma chyow*)

A literary way to say "flirt" or "banter flirtatiously." Literally "hit passionately, scold prettily" referring to the expression 打是亲骂是爱 **dǎ shì qīn mà shì ài** (*dah shih cheen ma shih aye*), which translates to something like "hitting is intimacy and yelling is love."

吃豆腐 **chī dòufu** (*chih doe foo*)

Cop a feel. Literally "eat tofu." When used between people of the same sex, it can mean "to bully," either verbally or physically. Used mainly in southern China, Taiwan, and Hong Kong, though northerners generally know the phrase as well. Relatedly, "sell tofu," 卖豆腐 **mài dòufu** (*my doe foo*), is a southern Chinese euphemism for prostitution.

泡妞 **pàonīu** (*pow nyoo*)

One of the most common slang terms for "hitting on," "flirting with," or "hooking up with" girls. Literally "soak a girl."

钓凯子 **diào kǎizi** (*dyow kigh dz*)

To pick up men, to hit on a man. Literally "fish for men" or "fish for a boyfriend." Originated in Taiwan and Hong Kong but known and used everywhere.

搭讪 **dā shàn** (*dah shahn*)

To chat someone up, to start up a conversation.

戏果戏孙 **xì guǒ xì sūn** (*she gwuh she swen*)

Beijing slang for "chasing girls and boys," or for people who go to bars with the express intent of finding a guy or girl to hook up with. 果 **Guǒ** (*gwuh*) means "fruit" but is Beijing slang for "chicks" because with a Beijing accent it's pronounced like 果儿 **guǒr** (*gwerr*). 戏果 **Xì guǒ** (*she gwuh*) literally means "play with chicks" or "trick girls" and is an old Beijing expression that means flirting with or hitting on girls. 戏孙 **Xì sūn** (*she swen*) literally means "trick boys" or "play with boys" and means hitting on or flirting with guys.

嗑蜜 **kē mì** (*kuh me*)

Beijing slang for "chasing" or "dating" women. Literally "hunt honey." Not as popular as **xì guǒ** (above).

扎蜜 **zhā mì** (*jah me*)

Beijing slang for "chasing women." Literally "fool around [with] honey." Not as popular as **xì guǒ** (page 56).

求爱 **qiúài** (*chyoe aye*)

Woo (intransitive verb). Literally "plead for love."

追求 **zhuīqiú** (*jway chyoe*)

To pursue (transitive verb).

垂涎三尺 **chuíxián sān chǐ** (*chway shin sahn chih*)

Literally "drool three feet." Said of something appealing that makes you drool. Mainly used in reference to food but can also be said of a girl.

眉来眼去 **méi lái yǎn qù** (*may lie yen chee*)

Literally "eyebrows coming and eyes going." Describes flirtatious eye contact or just flirting in general.

电眼 **diàn yǎn** (*dyinn yen*)

Literally "electric eyes." A popular term among young people to describe beguiling eyes—that is, eyes that give you an electric spark.

过电 **guò diàn** (*gwuh dyinn*) or 放电 **fàng diàn** (*fahng dyinn*)

To have an electric shock (in the sense of being attracted to someone). Literally "release electricity" and "pass electricity," respectively. Can also mean to knock the table with your glass when toasting, instead of clinking glasses.

来电 **lái diàn** (*lie dyinn*)

Romantic spark. Literally "electricity comes." Not having any chemistry would be 不来电 **bù lái diàn** (*boo lie dyinn*), literally "electricity doesn't come."

撒娇 **sǎjiāo** (*sah jow*)

To throw a fit, to act like a brat, to act coquettishly. The key thing to note in this definition is that acting coquettishly—that is, acting in a way that attracts male attention—is synonymous with acting like a brat.

耍单儿 **shuǎ dānr** (*shwah dar*)

Literally "play alone," meaning "single" or "unmarried," but also Beijing slang for dressing skimpily even though it's cold out, just to look cute.

漂亮 **piàoliang** (*pyow lyahng*)

Pretty. Can be said of someone who's actually pretty, like the girl next door, but is also said in response to anything impressive or amazing. This word is often used in sports—when a soccer player scores a goal, a westerner might say "Nice!" but in Chinese you often hear the sports commentators yell, "Pretty!"

美 **měi** (*may*) or 美丽 **měilì** (*may lee*)

Beautiful, good-looking. Can describe both people and things.

美女 **měi nǚ** (*may nee*)

Beautiful girl, beautiful woman. Often used as a flattering term of address.

甜 **tián** (*tyinn*)

Sweet. Can describe either food or girls. Its meaning differs from the English meaning "extremely nice and thoughtful" in that it also connotes "cutesy." For example, girls from Taiwan are described by mainlanders as sounding very **tián** because their accents sound girlish and cute to Chinese outside of Taiwan. A sweet girl is a 甜妞 **tián nīu** (*tyinn nyoo*).

可爱 **kě'ài** (*kuh aye*)

Cute.

卡哇依 **kǎwāyī** (*kuh why ee*)

Based on the Japanese word *kawaii*, meaning "cute" or "cutesy." Tends to be used more often in Taiwan and other areas more strongly influenced by Japanese culture.

娃娃 **wáwa** (*wah wah*—that should be a short *a*; rhymes with "tra-la-la")

Cute girl. Literally "baby" or "doll."

绝色 **juésè** (*dreh suh*)

An extremely beautiful appearance (used as a noun). Literally "special color." Used frequently on the Internet.

靓 **liàng** (*lyahng*)

Pretty or handsome. Literally "light" or "glowing" or "bright." A pretty girl is a 靓女 **liàng nǚ** (*lyahng nee*), literally "glowing girl," and a handsome young man is a 靓仔 **liàng zǎi**, literally "pretty boy." Used in southern China.

迷人 **mírén** (*me ren*)

Fascinating, enchanting, charming, tempting (usually describing a female). Literally "attracts people."

丰满 **fēngmǎn** (*fung mahn*)

Voluptuous, buxom. Literally "plentiful and full."

身材 **shēncái** (*shen tsigh*)

Figure, body. Literally "body shape."

条 **tiáo** (*tyow*)

Figure, shape (usually describing women). Ordinarily **tiáo** is a word that indicates reference to anything with a long and thin shape, like a stick or a noodle.

性感 **xìnggǎn** (*sheeng gahn*)

Sexy.

妖媚 **yāomèi** (*yow may*)

Sexy, enchanting. Literally "evil charming."

妖里妖气 **yāo lǐ yāo qì** (*yow lee yow chee*)

Seductive and bewitching, sexy.

妖精 **yāojing** (*yow jing*)

Alluring woman, siren. Literally "evil spirit."

尖果儿 **jiān guǒr** (*jinn gwurr*)

Beijing slang for a hot girl. Literally "sharp girl."

尖孙儿 **jiān sūnr** (*jinn swurr*)

Beijing slang for a hot guy. Literally "sharp guy."

辣妹 **làmèi** (*lah may*)

Southern Chinese slang for a hot girl. Literally "spicy sister."

惹火 **rěhuǒ** (*ruh hwuh*)

Sexy, hot (female). Popular among young people.

帅 **shuài** (*shwhy*—think of it as "shh" and "why" mushed into one syllable)

Handsome. Literally "leader in battle." Describes men, but like "pretty," **piàoliang** (page 59), this can also be said in re-

sponse to an impressive spectacle. You can make the sentiment stronger by saying 很帅! **hěn shuài!** (*hun shwhy*), literally "very handsome," or 帅呆了 **shuài dāi le**, literally
"stunningly handsome."

帅哥 **shuài gē** (*shwigh guh*—**shuài** rhymes with "high")

Handsome man. Literally "handsome older brother." Often
used as a flattering form of address for any good-looking
young man.

壮 **zhuàng** (*jwong*)

Buff, strong. Beijingers pronounce it using third tone instead
of fourth tone—**zhuǎng** (*jwong*).

酷 **kù** (*coo*)

Cool (a transliteration from the English). A common way to
describe a guy you find attractive, and more likely to be used
by young people today than 帅 **shuài** (*shwigh*), which means
"handsome."

棒 **bàng** (*bahng*—almost like "bong" but with an *ahh* sound
replacing the *o*)

Capable, strong, awesome. Often said when praising someone. If a child does a good job cleaning his or her room, you
can say 很棒! **hěn bàng!** (*hun bahng*), literally "very great." Or
if a girl has a really rockin' body, you can say,
"他的身材很棒!" "**Tā de shēncái hěn bàng!**" (*tah duh shen
tsigh hun bahng*): "Her body is awesome!"

倍儿棒 **bèir bàng** (*burr bahng*)

Really great, really awesome. This is how a Beijing or Tian-
jin local might express 棒 **bàng** (*bahng*). (倍 **Bèi** means

"multiply" and the 儿 er (*er*) sound indicates a Beijing accent.) Thus a Beijinger complimenting a girl's body might say, "你的身材倍儿棒!" "**Nǐ de shēncái bèir bang!**" (*nee duh shen tsigh burr bahng*): "You have a rockin' body."

养眼 **yǎngyǎn** (*yahng yen*)

Eye candy, good-looking, beautiful, easy on the eyes. Literally "fits eye."

喜欢 **xǐhuān** (*shee hwun*)

To like.

爱 **ài** (*aye*—rhymes with "sigh")

To love.

疼 **téng** (*tung*) or 疼爱 **téng ài** (*tung aye*)

Love (verb). Can be used both for romantic love and for parental or familial love. Can also mean "to spoil," as in spoiling a beloved child. **Téng** can also mean "pain," which you shouldn't read into too deeply, but knowing it should give extra depth to this way of saying love.

暗恋 **ànliàn** (*ahn lyinn*)

To have a crush on.

谈恋爱 **tánliàn'ài** (*tahn lyinn aye*)

To date, to have a relationship with. Literally "talk about love" or "talk romance."

约会 **yuēhuì** (*yreh hway*)

A date (noun). Came about due to Western influence.

AA 制 **AA zhì** (*AA jih*) and AB 制 **AB zhì** (*AB jih*)

Literally "AA system" and "AB system." "Going Dutch" when you eat out is often called **AA zhì** in Chinese. However, going Dutch is a relatively recent concept for Chinese people. More recently, some people (men dining out with women in particular) are choosing to split the bill but pay a bit more, say 70 percent, and this is called **AB zhì**.

初恋 **chūliàn** (*choo lyinn*)

First relationship, first love.

女朋友 **nǚpéngyǒu** (*nee pung yo*)

Girlfriend. A direct translation from the English word, and like the English it usually means the girl a guy is dating but sometimes merely refers to a female friend.

男朋友 **nánpéngyǒu** (*nahn pung yo*)

Boyfriend.

马子 **mǎzi** (*mah dz*)

A slangy word for "girlfriend." Originated in Hong Kong and was once used derogatorily (literally means "horse"), but now carries a positive connotation.

凯子 **kǎizi** (*kigh dz*)

A slangy term for "boyfriend" and the counterpart to **mǎzi** (above). Describes the ideal image of a boyfriend, as 凯 **kǎi** (*kigh*) means "triumphant" and connotes a hero victorious in battle.

我爱你 **wǒ ài nǐ** (*wuh aye nee*)

I love you.

鸳鸯 **yuānyāng** (*yren yahng*)

A pair of lovers. Also means Mandarin ducks, a frequent metaphor for lovers in classic literature.

拍拖 **pāituō** (*pie twuh*)

Courting, dating, being in love, having an affair. Literally "on patrol." Used in southern China.

热恋 **rèliàn** (*ruh lyinn*)

To be in the honeymoon phrase, head over heels.

蜜运 **mìyùn** (*mee yreen*)

Dating seriously. Literally "honey luck." When a man and woman are in a relationship likely headed toward marriage, young people might say that they are in **mìyùn**, or struck by "honey luck." The term is a play on the word "honeymoon," 蜜月 **mìyuè** (*mee yreh*), because they sound similar.

爱称 **àichēng** (*aye chung*)

Literally "love name." An affectionate nickname, like "baby" or "snookums." A few common Chinese "love names" are 宝贝 **bǎobèi** (*baow bay*), "baby" or "treasure"; 亲爱的 **qīnàide** (*cheen aye duh*), "dear" or "dearest" or "dear one"; 老公 **lǎogong** (*laow gohng*), "husband" but more literally "old husband"; and 老婆 **lǎopó** (*laow pwuh*), "wife" but more literally "old wife."

两小无猜 **liǎngxiǎowúcāi** (*lyahng shaow oo tsigh*)

Two innocent child playmates (puppy love).

青梅竹马 **qīngméizhúmǎ** (*cheeng may jooh mah*)

Childhood sweethearts. Literally "green plums and a bamboo horse," which are both references to childhood, as green plums are not yet ripe, and the bamboo horse refers to a childhood game of pretending to ride horses using a bamboo stick.

光棍节 **Guāng Gùn Jié** (*gwahng gwen jyih*)

Singles Day. A holiday probably invented by a bunch of Chinese college students in Nanjing during the 1990s, and held on November 11 because of all the ones in the date (11/11), which represent single people. On that date, at 11:11 p.m., male college students across China scream their desire for a girlfriend, bang on rice bowls with spoons, and otherwise make a lot of noise.

剩女 shèngnǔ (*shung nee*)

Literally "leftover woman." Refers to successful career women who have still not found a spouse, and who have passed an age that the Chinese consider ideal for getting married.

三隐女人 sān yǐn nǔrén (*sahn een nee ren*)

Literally "woman with three secrets." Refers to married women who, for whatever reasons, keep their marital status, age, and child a secret, leading everyone to think they're single.

一见钟情 yí jiàn zhōng qíng (*ee jinn johng cheeng*)

Love at first sight. Literally "see once and love." 锺情 **Zhōng qíng** (*johng ching*) means love or like.

爱屋及乌 ài wū jí wū (*aye ooh gee ooh*)

Literally "love house and bird." An expression meaning that when you love someone, you also love everything belonging to or associated with them. An equivalent English expression might be "Love me, love my dog."

空窗期 kōngchuāngqī (*kohng chwahng chee*)

Literally "open-window period," referring to the window of time after a breakup when a person is up for grabs. Used especially in reference to someone that everyone wants.

黄昏恋 huánghūnliàn (*hwahng hwen lyinn*) or 夕阳恋 xīyángliàn (*she yahng lyinn*)

Literally "love at dusk" or "sunset love." A romance between two elderly people. The rising sun is an oft-used metaphor for youth, and conversely the elderly are associated with the setting sun.

跨国恋 **kuàguóliàn** (*kwah gwuh lyinn*)

Literally "transnational love." Refers to a relationship between a Chinese person and a foreigner, or any intercultural relationship.

扛洋枪 **kángyángqiāng** (*kahng yahng chyahng*—the *ah* in all three syllables indicates a short *a*, as in "ma" or "la")

Literally "shoulder foreign rifles." Used in the late nineteenth century to refer to Chinese people using items from overseas (pens, clothes, etc.) and now refers to Chinese women who date and/or sleep with foreigners.

网恋 **wǎngliàn** (*wahng lyinn*)

Internet dating, falling in love via the Internet.

师生恋 **shī shēng liàn** (*shih shung lyinn*)

Literally "teacher-student love." A romantic relationship between a teacher and a student. Such relationships are extremely common in China, where it can be difficult for diligent students to meet romantic prospects.

老牛吃嫩草 **lǎoniú chī nèncǎo** (*low new chih nun tsow*)

A relationship between two people with a large age difference. Literally, "The old cow eats fresh grass."

姐弟恋 **jiědìliàn** (*jyih dee lyinn*)

A relationship between an older woman and a much younger man. Literally "older sister, younger brother love."

老少恋 **lǎoshàoliàn** (*laow shaow lyinn*)

Love between people with a big age difference. Literally "old-young love."

忘年恋 **wàngniánliàn** (*wahng nyinn lyinn*)

Being in love despite age differences. Literally "forgetting-age love."

两地恋 **liǎngdìliàn** (*lyahng dee lyinn*)

Long-distance relationship.

Miscellaneous types

傍大款 **bàngdàkuǎn** (*bahng dah kwahn*)

Literally "depend on a rich man" or "live off a rich man." Negatively describes a woman having an intimate relationship with a wealthy man who supports her (and who may or may not be already married).

味道美女 **wèidào měinǚ** (*way dow may nee*)

Hot waitress. Literally "delectable beauty."

骨头轻 **gǔtóu qīng** (*goo toe ching*)

Bimbo, airhead. Literally "light bones."

浪 **làng** (*lahng*)

Northern Chinese slang for "shallow," "airheaded," or "flighty" (describing women). Can also mean "to stroll" or "to wander."

绣花枕头 **xiùhuā zhěntou** (*show hwa jen toe*)

Literally "embroidered pillow," meaning something or someone that is beautiful but useless.

老来俏 **lǎo lái qiào** (*laow laow tsie*)

An older person who dresses young. Literally "[from] old to pretty."

装嫩 **zhuāng nèn** (*jwahng nun*)

Literally "pretending to be tender" or "faking softness" and describing someone who speaks girlishly, dresses young, and/or otherwise behaves much younger than he or she is.

校花 **xiàohuā** (*shyaow hwa*)

Literally "school flower." Equivalent to the head of the cheerleading team—the most popular and desired girl in school.

校草 **xiàocǎo** (*shaow tsow*—both syllables rhyme with "pow")

Literally "school grass." Equivalent to the high school quarterback—the school hunk.

后生 **hòushēng** (*ho shung*)

Young man. Literally "born later." Used in southern China.

滥情 **lànqíng** (*lahn cheeng*)

Something along the lines of a "romantic" crossed with a "player"—someone who loves everyone he or she sees. Said of both men and women. Literally "excessive feelings." Can be used as an adjective too, as in 他这人挺滥情的 **tā zhè rén** tǐng lànqíng de (*tah juh ren ting lahn ching duh*): literally "this person really has a lot of excessive feelings" but meaning something more like "this person's always falling in love with everyone he meets."

小白脸 **xiǎobáiliǎn** (*shyow buy lyinn*)

Literally "little white face." Refers to a young, slightly effeminate or somewhat "soft"-looking man (hence the white face, which is considered an effeminate feature). May also connote that the young man depends on an older woman for money instead of working for a living.

吃软饭 **chī ruǎnfàn** (*chih rwun fun*)

Literally "eat soft rice." A negative expression for a man (of any age) who depends on his girlfriend or wife for a living. Mainly used in southern China.

花 **huā** (*hwah*)

An adjective used to describe a "player." Literally "flower."

花花公子 **huāhuāgōngzǐ** (*hwa hwa gong dz*—the *gong* sound has a long *o*, like "oh")

A playboy (and also the Chinese name for *Playboy* magazine). Literally "flower prince."

钻石王老五 **zuànshí wáng lǎo wǔ** (*dzwun shih wahng low ooh*)

Literally "diamond bachelor." A wealthy, older, eligible man. Used mainly in Hong Kong and Taiwan (where it's written 鑽石王老五).

单身贵族 **dānshēn guì zú** (*dan shen gway dzoo*)

Literally "unmarried nobility." 单身 **Dānshēn** (*dan shen*) means "single" and many people now use this term with "nobility" added to convey the idea that there's nothing wrong with being single and it's something to be proud of, like something that noble people enjoy.

歪瓜劣枣 wāi guā liè zǎo (*why gwah lyih dzow*)

Literally "crooked melons and split-open dates," referring to a group of unattractive people. For example, 他们学校的男生都是些歪瓜劣枣 **Tā men xué xiào de nán shēng dōu shì xiē wāi guā liè zǎo** (*tah men shreh shaow duh nahn shung doe shih shih why gwah lyih dzow*) means "The boys at that school are all ugly."

娘娘腔 niángniangqiāng (*nyahng nyahng chyahng*)

Sissy, pansy, an effeminate man with a girly voice. Can imply that the person is gay, though can also be used teasingly with a close friend. Literally "girly tone."

奶油小生 nǎiyóu xiǎoshēng (*nigh yo shaow shung*)

An effeminate young man. Can be slightly derogatory, just like the word "girly." Literally "buttery young man" or "butter-boy."

夫妻相 fūqī xiàng (*foo chee shyung*)

Literally "husband-and-wife appearance." We often say that a husband and wife start to look like each other as time goes by. Somewhat along the same lines, many Chinese believe that a man and woman who share certain similar facial features will have a longer-lasting marriage, and thus matchmakers might consider their **fūqī xiàng** in debating their suitability for marriage.

王八看绿豆, 看对眼了 **wángbā kàn lǜdòu, kàn duì yǎn le**
(*wahng bah kahn lee dough, kahn dway yen luh*)

A joking expression that means two ugly people will find each other attractive. Literally "a tortoise will gaze at two mung beans" (because the eyes of a tortoise look like two mung beans).

情侣衫 **qínglǚ shān** (*cheeng lee shahn*) or 情侣装 **qínglǚ zhuāng** (*cheeng lee jwong*)

Matching couple outfits. Literally "lovers' shirts" or "couples' outfits." Also 对衫 **duì shān** (*dway shahn*), literally "matching shirts." There is an inexplicable trend in China (and also South Korea) of couples wearing matching shirts. One (of many) of these T-shirt sets has an arrow pointing toward the girl, and the words, "Falling in love, she is my girlfriend." The girl of course wears a shirt with an arrow pointing to the man, which says, "Falling in love, he is my boyfriend." Moreover, these couples somehow manage to stay on the correct side of each other, always, while walking, sitting, shopping, and eating, so that the arrows are always pointing at each other.

闪约 **shǎnyuē** (*shan yreh*)
Speed-dating. Literally "flash appointment."

Marriage

闪婚 **shǎnhūn** (*shahn hwen*)
Literally "flash marriage," describing couples who meet, fall in love, and get married very quickly.

两地分居 **liǎng dì fēn jū** (*lyahng dee fen gee*)

Long-distance marriage. Literally "in two different places" or "in two different cities." Such marriages have long been common in China due to a strict residence permit system that results in many people finding work in cities far from their spouse, though nowadays this situation is improving.

金龟婿 **jīnguī xù** (*jean gway she*)

A rich husband. Literally "golden turtle husband." A golden turtle was a status symbol denoting high rank for officials in the Tang dynasty (618–907).

半糖夫妻 **bàntáng fūqī** (*bahn tahng foo chee*)

Literally "half-sweet couple." Couples who live apart during the work week and only spend weekends together, to keep the romance alive in their marriage. An increasingly common phenomenon among upper-middle-class professionals.

走婚族 **zǒuhūn zú** (*dzoe hwen dzoo*—the first syllable rhymes with Joe but with the beginning sound like a *d* and *z* slurred together)

Literally "walking marriage." Used to describe young Chinese couples in big cities who stay with their respective parents during the work week and live together only during the weekend.

急婚族 **jíhūn zú** (*gee hwen dzoo*)

Literally "hasty marriage group." A new term that describes people who marry hastily and not for love, especially young women who marry a wealthy man soon after graduating from college so they don't have to work.

形式结婚 **xíngshì jiéhūn** (*sheeng shih jyih hwen*)

A marriage of convenience—for example, between a gay man and a lesbian.

二锅头 **èrguōtóu** (*er gwuh toe*)

Literally "second-pot head" and the name of a brand of twice-distilled Chinese liquor. Also slang for a woman who remarries.

Love's downsides

抬杠 **táigàng** (*tie gahng*)

Beijing slang for arguing for the sake of argument or for no reason. Also means being unreasonable in an argument, or deliberately picking a (verbal) fight. Literally "lifting the pole," as in someone who keeps lifting up one end of the scale just to be higher than the other.

堕入情网 **duò rù qíng wǎng** (*dwuh roo cheeng wahng*)

Lovesick. Literally "sink into love's net."

麦芽糖女人 **màiyátáng nǔrén** (*migh yah tahng nee ren*)

Literally "malt sugar women." Refers to possessive women who demand that their boyfriends or husbands spend every second with them—cling to them like sticky malt sugar.

气管炎 **qìguǎnyán** (*chee gwun yen*)

Literally "lung infection." Refers to a man who is so whipped that he never talks back to his girlfriend or wife, thus his friends might jokingly say he has a lung infection.

见光死 **jiàn guāng sǐ** (*gin gwahng sih*)

Literally "killed by exposure to light." Refers to two people who fall for each other via the Internet or phone dates, but whose would-be romance is sadly killed by the cold, harsh light of reality once they actually meet.

离婚同居 **líhūn tóngjū** (*lee hwen tohng gee*)

Continuing to live together after a divorce, either because one or both sides can't afford a new home or because they refuse to pay their ex for their half of the home they jointly owned before the divorce.

断背婚姻 **duànbèi hūnyīn** (*dwun bay hwen een*)

Literally "brokeback marriage," after the Ang Lee movie *Brokeback Mountain*. Refers to a marriage in which one side is gay and/or has had a gay affair.

私房钱 **sīfángqián** (*sih fahng chyinn*)

Literally "private house money." Refers to the secret stash of money that a wife puts aside in case her husband leaves her. Also refers to the money that a husband secretly puts outside of his wife's reach because he's whipped and is expected to give her all the money he earns.

吃醋 **chīcù** (*chih tsoo*)

To be jealous, to be envious. Literally "to eat vinegar." A 醋坛子 **cù tánzi** (*tsoo tahn dz*), literally "vinegar jar," is a jealous person.

窝里横 **wōlǐhèng** (*wuh lee hung*)

Literally "unruly in the nest," referring to people who seem polite and civilized in public and only reveal their nastiness at home.

三角恋 **sānjiǎo liàn** (*sahn jow lyinn*)

Love triangle.

爱恨交加 **ài hèn jiāojiā** (*aye hun jow jah*)

Love-hate relationship.

心碎 **xīn suì** (*sheen sway*)

Brokenhearted.

反目成仇 **fǎn mù chéng chóu** (*fun moo chung cho*)

Utter hatred after a breakup.

Extramarital affairs

有一腿 **yǒu yì tuǐ** (*yo ee tway*)

Have an affair. Literally "has one leg," suggesting a man's leg intertwined with a woman's. Originated in Hong Kong or Taiwan but used everywhere.

劈腿 **pī tuǐ** (*pee tway*)

Affair, cheat, two-timing. Literally "split legs." Also the technical term for a split in gymnastics. Commonly used in southern China.

戴绿帽子 **dài lǜmàozi** (*die lee mao dz*)

A cuckold, a man who is being cheated on. Literally "wear a green hat," supposedly because male-brother workers during the Tang dynasty had to wear green hats. Because of this term, no Chinese man, and even many Chinese women, will wear green hats. One friend of mine found this out when he had to organize an office Christmas party, and all the Chinese in the office shot down his idea of dressing like elves, as it meant they'd have to wear green hats.

负心汉 **fù xīn hàn** (*foo sheen hahn*)

Cheater (referring to a man). Literally "cheating man."

包二奶 **bāoèrnǎi** (*bow er nigh*—the *bow* sound rhymes with "cow") or just 二奶 **èrnǎi** (*er nigh*)

Long ago, when Chinese men had multiple wives, **èrnǎi** referred to the second wife. Today it refers to the mistresses of wealthy men and government officials, an extremely common fact of life in China. Literally "packaged second wife."

傍家儿 **bàng jiār** (*bahng jer*)

Mistress. Literally "depend on home." Pejorative term for a young woman who has an affair with a rich married man. Used in Beijing only.

榜肩 **bàng jiàn** (*bahng jyinn*)

Beijing slang for an extramarital lover. Literally "depend on shoulders."

情儿 **qíngr** (*churr*)

Beijing slang for an extramarital lover. Literally "passion."

小老婆 **xiǎolǎopó** (*shyaow laow pwuh*)

Mistress. Literally "little wife."

蜜 **mì** (*me*) or 小蜜 **xiǎo mì** (*shyow me*)

Mistress. Literally "honey" or "little honey."

婚外恋 **hūnwàiliàn** (*hwen why lyinn*)

Extramarital love.

小三 **xiǎo sān** (*shyow sahn*)

Literally "little third." Refers to the "third person" in a relationship; i.e., the mistress.

出位 **chū wèi** (*choo way*)

Literally "overstep the mark." Describes a person who has had an extramarital affair. May also describe other situations when a person inappropriately "oversteps the mark"—for example, job applicants who include sexually provocative photos of themselves in their resume (a not infrequent phenomenon, as it is legal for employers in China to require that applicants submit a photo, and many even require that girls be within a certain height and weight limit).

漂婚 **piāo hūn** (*pyow hwen*)

A fake marriage, of sorts, between two people who are already married to other people, but who manage to establish a life like they are married in another town. This phenomenon is made easier by the fact that many Chinese wind up living and working far away from their spouses due to a strict residence permit system. Literally "floating marriage."

亚偷情 **yā tōu qíng** (*yah toe cheeng*)

Literally "second stolen feelings." Refers to married people who have an intense friendship with a friend of the opposite sex and are so close that they are practically having an affair, but without ever actually having sex.

CHAPTER FIVE

Sex and Body Parts

For much of China's four thousand years of history, sex was an open topic studied and perfected in great detail. Ancient Taoists believed that immortality (or, at the very least, longevity) could be achieved through sex, and medical texts dating as far back as the second century BC have been found to treat sex as an academic field of study. Specific sexual positions with names like Flying Dragon and Jumping Monkey were recommended to treat specific ailments, and illustrated sex manuals were kept by the bed for easy reference and sometimes even given as gifts to new brides. Women were considered to have an inexhaustible supply of yin, a sort of cosmic life essence, and men could replenish their own limited supply of that essence (in them called yang) by inducing a woman to multiple orgasm while refraining from ejaculating themselves, thereby drawing in the woman's energy. Yin and yang also represented female and male sexual parts. Some texts recommended sex with as many as ten different women in a night; others extolled the life-extending virtues of sex with virgins, ideally no older than fourteen.

The puritan ethics of, first, Confucianism (which, among its many other codes of conduct, dictated that a man and a woman should never touch in public) and, then, Communism (which kept marital sex hidden and outlawed extra- and premarital sex) effectively wiped out such open discourse. But ever since the period of "reform and opening," beginning with the controversy surrounding new China's first published photo of a kiss in 1979, sex has steadily become a more and more open topic. Today there are sex shops all over the place, the pickup scene in bars late at night looks pretty much the same as anywhere else in the world, and men across the country, either suffering from erectile dysfunction or just wanting to perk up their sex lives, are snapping up all the caterpillar fungus, deer penis, and Viagra they can get.

Nonetheless, China officially remains an extremely conservative society when it comes to sex. Dating and public displays of affection are frowned upon or even outright banned on many college campuses; TV shows and movies depict women in their late twenties who still live at home in rooms filled with stuffed animals; and a Taiwanese actress who appeared in Ang Lee's NC-17-rated *Lust, Caution* has been blackballed from the mainland media.

However, one need only to stroll through the public parks of China at dusk, when every bench and shadow is occupied by ardent young couples strenuously making out (or more), to be reminded that despite the best efforts of China's sternest cock blockers, nothing will ever keep the birds and the bees apart. To that end, here are the words that help make China the world's most populous country.

Virginity

处女 **chǔnǚ** (*choo nee*)

Virgin (female).

处男 **chǔnán** (*choo nahn*)

Virgin (male).

黄花闺女 **huáng huā guīnǚ** (*hwahng hwun gway nee*)

Virgin (female). Literally "yellow flower girl," alluding to a fashion during the Song dynasty when girls would decorate their faces with yellow plum flowers. When these flowers were not in bloom, they used yellow paper cutouts instead.

雏 **chú** (*choo*)

Dirty and/or insulting Beijing slang for a virgin. Literally "chick" or "young bird." Before 1949 this was frequently used in brothels to refer to a young prostitute without much experience in entertaining the customers: "chicken" is slang for a prostitute, so a "chick" would be a young prostitute.

破雏 **pò chú** (*pwuh choo*)

Insulting and/or lewd Beijing slang for losing one's virginity. Literally "break chick."

破处 **pò chǔ** (*pwuh choo*)

To lose one's virginity. Literally "break virginity."

开包 **kāi bāo** (*kigh baow—kigh* rhymes with "high")

Beijing slang for losing one's virginity. Literally "open the package."

Lust

性欲冲动 **xìngyù chōngdòng** (*shing yee chohng dohng*)

Arousal, sexual desire. 性欲 **Xìngyù** (*shing yee*) can also be used by itself to mean "lust" or "desire," while 冲动 **chōngdòng** (*chohng dohng*) alone is literally "impulse" but can mean horny or aroused.

闹春 **nào chūn** (*now chren*)

Sexual arousal, lust. Literally "noise in springtime."

欲火焚身 **yù huǒ fén shēn** (*yee hwuh fen shen*)

Sexual arousal, lust. Literally "the fire of lust is burning in the body."

饥渴 **jī kě** (*gee kuh*)

Literally "hungry and thirsty." Can be used in many different contexts to mean that someone is hungry for something, such as knowledge. In a sexual context, it suggests that someone is starving for sex.

发春 **fāchūn** (*fah chren*)

Horny (the most straightforward equivalent to the English). Literally "to develop spring" or "life" or "lust."

发情 **fāqíng** (*fah cheeng*)

Horny. Applies mostly to animals but sometimes said of people in a joking way. Literally "develop passion."

发骚 **fāsāo** (*fah saow*—**sāo** rhymes with "cow")

A vulgar and impolite way to say "horny." Literally "to develop sexy/slutty."

发浪 **fālàng** (*fah lahng*)

Horny (although more usually means "slutty"). Literally "unrestrained." Not as current as the other three terms above, though still commonly used.

Masturbation

手淫 **shǒuyín** (*show een*)

Masturbate, masturbation (technical term). Literally "hand lewdness."

自慰 **zìwèi** (*dz way*)

Masturbate, masturbation (technical term). Literally "self-comfort."

自渎 **zìdú** (*dz do*)

Masturbate, masturbation (technical term). Literally "self-abuse."

打飞机 **dǎfēijī** (*dah fay gee*)

The most common slang term for "jerk off" or "hand job." Literally "shoot airplanes."

玩老二 **wán lǎoèr** (*wahn laow er*)

Jerk off, hand job. Literally "play with little brother."

打手枪 **dǎ shǒuqiāng** (*da show chyahng*)

Jerk off, hand job. Literally "fire the gun." More commonly used in southern China than in the North.

手推 **shǒutuī** (*show tway*)

Jerk off, hand job. Literally "hand push."

撸 **lū** (*loo*)

Refers to any sort of sliding or rubbing movement done on something else: for example the action of removing a ring from a finger. Can also be a euphemism for jerking off.

射 **shè** (*shuh*)

Cum, come. The most common, colloquial way to refer to 射精 **shèjīng** (*shuh jing*), which literally means "shoot sperm" and is the formal term for "ejaculation" (noun) or "ejaculate" (verb).

泄精 **xièjīng** (*shyih jing*)

Premature or accidental ejaculation. For example, during a wet dream or when about to have sex. Literally "leak semen."

精液 **jīngyè** (*jing yeh*)

Semen.

DIY

Female masturbation (said in English.) Short for "do it yourself." Used more commonly among lesbians, though may refer to any sort of female masturbation.

自摸 **zìmō** (*dz mwuh*)

Female masturbation. Literally "rub self." This is originally a mahjong term referring to a player taking a card from the stack on the table instead of from another player.

假鸡巴 **jiǎ jība** (*jah gee bah*)

Dildo. Literally "fake dick."

电动机巴 **diàndòng jība** (*dyinn dohng gee bah*)

Vibrator. Literally "electric dick."

Foreplay

亲吻 **qīnwěn** (*cheen when*) and 亲嘴 **qīnzuǐ** (*cheen dzway*—the second syllable is a tough one: pronounce a *z* sound while your mouth and tongue are in the position to pronounce the letter *d* and then continue into the word "way")

Kiss. Literally "touch lips" and "touch mouths," respectively. 亲 **Qīn** (*cheen*) or 吻 **wěn** (*when*) can also be used alone to mean "kiss."

舌吻 **shéwěn** (*shuh when*)

French kiss. Literally "tongue kiss."

啃 **kěn** (*ken*)

To kiss in a deep, wild way involving a lot of teeth. Literally means "nibble" or "gnaw."

咬咬 **yǎoyǎo** (*yow yow*)

Bite.

种草莓 **zhòng cǎoméi** (*johng tsow may*)

Give a hickey. Literally "plant a strawberry." Popular among people in their twenties or younger.

咖喱鸡 **gālíjī** (*gah lee gee*)

Hickey. Literally "curry chicken."

前戏 **qiánxì** (*chyinn she*)

Foreplay.

前奏 **qiánzòu** (*chyinn dzoe*)

Foreplay. Literally "prelude."

奶罩 **nǎizhào** (*nigh jow*)

A more vulgar way of saying "bra." It's not dirty and is fine to say among friends, but you wouldn't use this, for example, when speaking with a sales clerk in a lingerie store.

丁字裤 **dīngzì kù** (*ding dz koo*)

Thong. Literally "Ding character underwear," or underwear shaped like the character for the Chinese surname Ding: 丁.

Breasts

波波 **bōbō** (*bwuh bwuh*) or just 波 **bō** (*bwuh*)

Boobs (based on the sound of the English word "boobs").

咪咪 **mīmi** (*me me*)

Boobs. **Mīmi** is also Chinese onomatopoeia for the sound of a cat's meow. Mainly used in southern China.

奶奶 **nǎinǎi** (*nigh nigh*) or 奶子 **nǎizi** (*nigh dz*)

A cutesy/childish way of saying breasts (like "boobies"). Used in Taiwan and southern China only: **nǎinǎi** means "grandmother" in northern China.

杂儿 **zá'er** (*dzer*)

Tits. Beijing slang only and considered quite dirty.

馒头 **mántóu** (*mahn toe*)

Northern Chinese slang for "boobs." Literally "steamed bun," a Chinese staple food that resembles a bread roll.

巨无霸 **jùwúbà** (*gee oo bah*)

The Chinese name for a Big Mac and also slang for huge breasts.

乳头 **rǔtóu** (*roo toe*)

Nipple. Literally "breast head."

乳尖 **rǔjiān** (*roo gin*)

Tits (slightly vulgar).

波霸 **bōbà** (*bwuh bah*)

A woman with huge breasts. A slightly comical term, as 霸 **bà** (*bah*) describes something overwhelming, and so the literal meaning is "overwhelming breasts." From southern China.

飞机场 **fēijīchǎng** (*fay gee chahng*)

Flat-chested woman. Literally "airport" (because an airplane runway is very flat). A frequently used term.

太平公主 **tàipíng gōngzhǔ** (*tie peeng gohng joo*)

A teasing and frequently used term for a flat-chested girl. Literally "very flat princess."

搓板 **cuōbǎn** (*tswuh bahn*)

Literally "washboard," referring to a skinny, flat-chested girl.

乳交 **rǔjiāo** (*roo jow*)

Titty fuck, boob sex.

三点全露 **sān diǎn quán lòu** (*san dyinn chren low*)

Literally "three points all showing," meaning full-frontal nudity. Often used to describe a naked woman.

Oral Sex

口交 **kǒujiāo** (*koe jow*)

Oral sex (scientific term, not slang).

口活 **kǒuhuó** (*koe hwuh*)

Slang for oral sex (both male and female). Among several other possible translations, can be literally interpreted as "mouth life" or "mouth living" or "mouth work."

吹箫 **chuīxiāo** (*chway shaow*)

Blow job, give a blow job. Literally "play the bamboo flute."

吹口琴 **chuī kǒuqín** (*chway koe cheen*)

A euphemism for giving oral sex to a woman. Literally "play the harmonica." Not terribly common, but you will encounter at least a few people who have heard this. Even if they haven't, for Chinese ears this is one of those terms that just "makes sense" when you hear it.

舔屄 **tiǎn bī** (*tyinn bee*)

Lick pussy. Not an actual term, exactly, but many people don't know of any slang for going down on a girl, and this is a way to discuss it that anyone will understand.

舔舔下边 **tiǎn tiǎn xiàbiān** (*tyinn tyinn shah byinn*)

Literally "lick below" or "lick down there." Again, not an actual term but a useful way to describe something for which there aren't any universally known slang terms (and less dirty than the previous entry).

吹喇叭 **chuī lǎba** (*chway lah bah*)

Blow job, give a blow job. Literally "blow the horn."

吃香蕉 **chī xiāngjiāo** (*chih shyahng jow*)

Blow job, give a blow job. Literally "eat banana." More common in Taiwan, Hong Kong, and southern China, and mostly unknown in the North.

指交 **zhǐjiāo** (*jih jow*)

Fingering. Literally "finger sex."

湖吹 **húchuǐ** (*who chway*)

Fingering to wet climax. Literally "lake blast." A term from Japanese porn, and not something you'll likely encounter in regular speech.

Sex!

性 **xìng** (*shing*)

Sex.

性交 **xìngjiāo** (*shing jow*)

Have sex.

性爱 **xìngài** (*shing aye*)

A literary term for "sexual love" or "passion."

鱼水之欢 **yú shuǐ zhī huān** (*ee shway jhh hwun*—**zhī** is tricky: say "shh" while your mouth is in the position for making a *j* sound)

A euphemism for sex in use since ancient times. Literally, "The fish and the water are happy together," from the play *Romance of the West Chamber* by the Yuan dynasty playwright Wang Shifu (1260–1336).

Guītóu

云雨 **yúnyǔ** (*een yee*)

A euphemism for sex in use since ancient times. Literally "clouds and rain." Based on an ancient Chinese conception of heaven and earth mating during a rain storm (an image frequently used in erotic Chinese literature). "Rain" represents the man's semen, and "clouds" the woman's vaginal secretions.

翻云覆雨 **fān yún fù yǔ** (*fun een foo yee*—there is no hard *y* in the *yee* sound; it sounds closer to *ee* but with a very soft *y* at the beginning: the mouth should only be partially in the position to pronounce a *y*)

A euphemism for sex in use since ancient times, with the same origins as the entry above. Literally "turning clouds and overflowing water."

行房 **xíng fáng** (*shing fahng*)

A euphemism for having sex. Literally, something like "go to the room."

同房 **tóngfáng** (*tohng fahng*)

A euphemism for "sleeping together." Can also mean "live together." Literally "sharing a room" or "share a house."

交合 **jiāo hé** (*jow huh*)

"Get together."

那个 **nèigè** (*nay guh*)

Literally "that" but can serve as a euphemism for sex for anyone too embarrassed to use **zuò'ài** (page 93), and much like saying "it" or "you know what" in English. Thus you might say, "她已经跟我那个了" "**Tā yíjīng gēn wǒ nèigè le**" (*tah ee jing gehn tah nay guh luh*): "She did it with me."

做爱 **zuò'ài** (*zwuh aye*)

Make love.

做 **zuò** (*dzwuh*)

To do, to make. A euphemism for having sex. Similar to "doing" someone or saying they "do it" in English.

弄 **nòng** (*nohng*)

Do, mess with.

收 **shōu** (*show*)

Beijing slang for "have sex." Used similarly to "do." Literally "receive." Also a decent approximation for the term "hook up."

炒饭 **chǎofàn** (*chow fahn*)

Literally "fried rice." Taiwan slang for having sex (written 炒飯 in Taiwan), because stir-frying rice involves a lot of flipping and turning.

插 **chā** (*cha*)

Bang. A dirty way to say "have sex." Literally "insert."

打炮 **dǎpào** (*dah pow*)

Literally "blasting cannons" or "shooting shells." Dirty northern Chinese slang for having sex.

干 **gān** (*gahn*)

Fuck, do. A dirty way to refer to sex. Some example usages include 你干了她? **Nǐ gān le tā**? (*nee gahn luh ta*), "Did you do her?" and 你和他干了？ **Nǐ hé tā gān le**? (*nee huh tah gahn luh*): "Did you do it with him?"

搞 **gǎo** (*gaow*)

Screw, fuck, do. A dirty word for sex, though less dirty than **gān** (above). Example usages: 他乱搞男女关系！ **Tā luàn gǎo nǎnnǚ guānxì**！(*tah lwen gaow nahn nee gwahn she*), "He's been screwing someone!" (literally, "He's been indiscriminately doing male-female relations"); or 我要搞她！ **Wǒ yào gǎo tā!** (*wuh yow gaow ta*): "I want to fuck her!"

搞一下 **gǎo yīxià** (*gaow ee shah*)

Literally "do once" or "do for a short while." Can also be used similarly to "hooking up," although there is no Chinese term that fully matches the English.

夃 **cào**, more commonly written 操 **cāo** (both pronounced *tsow*)

Fuck. The character 夃 is visually quite graphic, as it is composed of 入 **rù** (*roo*), "enter," and 肉 **ròu** (*row*), "meat." 夃 is technically the correct character for "fuck," but because it is not included in most computer or phone-character input systems, and because it's just so uncomfortably dirty looking, most people write the homophonous 操 (which actually means "hold"). 夃 **Cào** / 操 **cāo** is mainly used for swearing—for example 夃你妈! **Cào nǐ mā!** (*tsow nee ma*), which means "Fuck your mother!" or "Fuck you"—and not usually to describe actual sex. If it is used in the context of actual sex, it's extremely dirty and also very derogatory.

日 **rì** (*rih*)

Southern Chinese slang for "fuck." Its usage is the same as **cào** above—it is extremely dirty and used mainly for swearing, not to describe sex. Also used a bit in a few northern areas like Shan'xi and Shandong provinces.

419

One-night stand (pronounced in English). Used because "four one nine" sounds like "for one night," and also because the Chinese pronunciation of those numbers, **sìyāojiǔ** (*sih yow joe*), sounds similar to 睡一宿 **shuì yī xiǔ** (*shway ee show*), which means "sleep one night." Used in mainland China only.

套子 **tàozi** (*taow dz*) or 套套 **tào tao** (*taow taow*)
Cutesy ways of saying "condom."

Male genitalia

阴茎 **yīnjīng** (*een jing*)
Penis.

阳具 **yángjù** (*yahng gee*)
Dick. Literally "sex tool." Used a lot in erotic writing and pornographic novels but not in speech.

玉茎 **yùjīng** (*yee jing*)

Literally "jade stalk." A poetic euphemism for "penis," dating to ancient times. Not used in speech.

鸡巴 **jība** (*gee bah*)

Cock, dick. The most common slang word for a penis, and quite vulgar. Also used as an intensifier in the same way you'd use a swear word: for example, "that **jība** whore" is stronger than simply "that whore."

鸡鸡 **jī ji** (*gee gee*) or 小鸡鸡 **xiǎo jī ji** (*shaow gee gee*)

A cutesy term for "penis," used by little kids or jokingly between lovers. Literally "chick" and "little chick," respectively. Often written "JJ" online.

老二 **lǎo'èr** (*laow er*—rhymes with "cow " and "her")

Dick. Literally "second brother" or "little brother."

小弟弟 **xiǎo dì di** (*shyow dee dee*—**xiǎo** rhymes with "cow ")

A kiddie term for "penis," much like "peenie" or "wee-wee." Literally "little brother."

屌 **diǎo** (*dyow*), sometimes written 吊 **diào** (*dyow*)

Dick, cock. Used more as an insult than to actually refer to a penis.

鸟 **niǎo** (*nyow,* rhymes with "cow ")

Dick, cock. Literally "bird." Less common than **diǎo** (above).

命根子 **mìng gēnzi** (*ming gehn dz*—that's a hard *g* in **gēn**, like the *g* in "get")

Euphemism for "penis," literally meaning "root of life," "lifeblood," or "one's own life." An extremely formal and/or literary term, but sometimes used jokingly in colloquial speech.

割包皮 **gēbāopí** (*guh baow pee*)

Circumcised, circumcision (which is rare in China). "Are you circumcised?" is 你割包皮没有? **Nǐ gēbāopí méiyǒu?** (*nee guh baow pee may yo*).

鸡巴毛 **jībamáo** (*gee bah maow*)

Literally "dick hair." A crude term for male pubic hair. Used more as an insult than to actually refer to pubic hair, for which the neutral term is 阴毛 **yīnmáo** (*een mao*—**máo** rhymes with "cow.")

yú shuǐ zhī huān

龟头 **guītóu** (*gway toe*)

Scientific term for the glans, or head of the penis. Literally "tortoise head."

包皮 **bāopí** (*baow pee*—**bāo** rhymes with "cow")

Foreskin. Literally "wrapper" or "wrap skin."

睾丸 **gāowán** (*gaow wahn*—**gāo** rhymes with "cow" and **wán** sounds like the "won" in "wonton soup")

Formal term for testicles.

蛋 **dàn** (*dahn*) or 蛋蛋 **dàn dàn** (*dahn dahn*)

Balls. Literally "eggs."

得儿 **de'r** (*durr*)

Beijing slang for "balls." This term is so colloquial that most Beijingers don't know how to write it, so don't be too concerned with the characters for this one.

勃起 **bóqǐ** (*bwuh chee*)

Have an erection, erection.

直 **zhí** (*jih*)

Hard. Literally "straight" or "vertical" or "upright."

硬 **yìng** (*eeng*) or 硬了 **yìng le** (*eeng luh*)

Hard, get hard.

铁硬 **tiě yìng** (*tyih eeng*)

Rock hard (referring to an erection). Literally "iron hard."

Female genitalia

阴道 **yīndào** (*een dow*)

Vagina. Literally "female path."

阴户 **yīnhù** (*een who*)

Poetic/literary term for the vagina. Literally "female door."

下身 **xiàshēn** (*shah shen*) or 下体 **xiàtǐ** (*shah tee*)

Euphemism for the female private parts. Literally "lower body."

小妹妹 **xiǎo mèimei** (*shyaow may may*)

Most common slang term for "vagina." Literally "little sister."

屄 **bī** (*bee*)

Cunt, pussy (extremely dirty). Often written 逼 instead, which means "compel" or "close" but is pronounced the same (and looks less dirty).

屄毛 **bīmáo** (*bee maow*)

A dirty term for female pubic hair.

白虎 **báihǔ** (*by who*)

Shaved pussy. Literally "white tiger." In ancient times **báihǔ** meant a woman with no pubic hair, shunned by matchmakers because it was believed that such a woman would bring misfortune or even death to her husband. The male equivalent is 青龙 **qīnglong** (*cheen lohng*), literally "green dragon," meaning a man without pubic hair, also superstitiously believed to bring trouble or death to his wife.

阴蒂 **yīndì** (*een dee*)
Clitoris.

湿 **shī** (*shih*)
Wet.

出水 **chū shuǐ** (*choo shway*)
Release vaginal secretions, get wet. Literally "discharge water."

淫水 **yínshuǐ** (*een shway*)
Cunt juice. Literally "lewd juice."

屄水 **bīshuǐ** (*bee shway*)
Cunt juice. Literally "pussy water."

Buttocks

屁股 **pìgǔ** (*pee goo*)
Butt.

腚 **dìng** (*ding*)
Butt.

股沟 **gǔgōu** (*goo go*)
Butt crack.

肛门 **gāngmén** (*gahng men*)

Anus.

屁眼 **pìyǎn** (*pee yen*)

Asshole (as in the slang term for "anus" but, unlike the English, is not used as an insult). Literally "butt eye."

菊花门 **júhuāmén** (*gee hwa men*) or just 菊花 **júhuā** (*gee hwa*)

Anus. Literally "chrysanthemum door" or just "chrysanthemum," because the anus resembles a chrysanthemum flower. Used a lot in erotic writing and pornographic novels, which tend to use poetic euphemisms for sex and body parts, but not used in speech.

肛交 **gāngjiāo** (*gahng jow*)

Anal sex.

鸡奸 **jījiān** (*gee gin*)

Ass fucking. 鸡 **jī** (*gee*) means "chicken" and 奸 **jiān** (*gin*) is a derogatory word for sex, though it's not obscene like "fucking."

走后门 **zǒuhòumén** (*dzoe hoe men*)

Go the back way—a euphemism for having anal sex. Has a slightly humorous edge because this is also an extremely common term in everyday speech that means "pulling strings," or using one's connections or other unofficial channels to get something done.

Orgasm

高潮 **gāocháo** (*gaow chow*)
Orgasm (noun).

来 **lái** (*lie*)
Come (both noun and verb). The colloquial term for an orgasm in northern China.

去 **qù** (*chee*)
The colloquial term for an orgasm (both noun and verb) in southern China and Taiwan, which interestingly is the exact opposite of the northern term, as it literally means "go."

颜射 **yánshè** (*yen shuh*)
Facial (cum in face). Literally "face eject." A term from Japanese porn (the characters are the same in Japanese).

Sexual positions

传教士式 **chuánjiàoshì shì** (*chren jow shih shih*)
Missionary. A literal translation from the English.

小狗式 **xiǎogǒu shì** (*shyaow go shih*), or less commonly
狗爬式 **gǒupá shì** (*go pah shih*)
Doggie-style.

侧进式 **cè jìn shì** (*tsuh gene shih*)
Spooning. Literally "enter from one side."

女上男下式 **nǚ shàng nán xià shì** (*nee shahng nahn shah shih*)
Cowgirl. Literally "woman on top, man underneath."

仙姑划船 **xiāngū huáchuán** (*shin goo hwah chwun*)
Cowgirl. Literally "goddess rowing the boat."

女上男下变式 **nǚ shàng nán xià biàn shì** (*nee shahng nahn shah byinn shih*)
Reverse cowgirl. Literally "woman on top, man underneath, switched."

莲花坐式 **liánhuā zuò shì** (*lyinn hwa dzwuh shih*)
Lotus position.

69 式 **liù jiǔ shì** (*lew joe shih—* **liù** rhymes with "ew")
Sixty-nine.

Alternative types of sex

电话性爱 **diànhuà xìng'ài** (*dyinn hwa shing aye*)
Phone sex.

网络性爱 **wǎngluò xìng'ài** (*wahng lwuh shing aye*)
Internet sex.

三人行 **sān rén xíng** (*sahn ren sheeng*)
Threesome. Literally "three people walking," a takeoff on a famous Confucian saying: "三人行，必有我师也" "**Sān rén xíng, bì yǒu wǒ shī yě**" (*sahn ren sheeng, bee yow uh shih yeh*):

"Among any three people walking together, there is always one you can learn from."

三 P / 3P **sān P** (*sahn P*)

Threesome. Literally "three P." The P stands for "people" or "person."

群交 **qún jiāo** (*chreen jow*)

Group sex, orgy.

拳插 **quán chā** (*chren cha*)

Fisting. Literally "fist inserts."

恋物癖 **liàn wù pì** (*lyinn oo pee*)

Fetish. Literally "love thing hobby."

恋足癖 **liàn zú pì** (*lyinn dzoo pee*)

Foot fetish.

恋声癖 **liàn shēng pì** (*lyinn shung pee*)

Sound fetish.

恋兽癖 **liàn shòu pì** (*lyinn show pee*)

Bestiality.

恋鞋癖 **liàn xié pì** (*lyinn shyih pee*)

Shoe fetish.

恋尸癖 **liàn shī pì** (*lyinn shih pee*)

Necrophilia.

恋袜癖 **liàn wà pì** (*lyinn wah pee*)

Sock or stocking fetish. Literally "loving socks hobby" or "love stockings habit."

恋手癖 **liàn shǒu pì** (*lyinn show pee*)

Hand fetish.

恋乳癖 **liàn rǔ pì** (*lyinn roo pee*)

Breast fetish.

恋衣癖 **liàn yī pì** (*lyinn ee pee*)

Clothing fetish.

虐恋 **nüè liàn** (*nyreh lyinn*)

S-M, sadomasochism. Literally "cruel love."

SM 女 **SM nǚ** ("SM" *nee*)

Dominatrix. Literally "S-M woman."

打屁股 **dǎ pìgu** (*dah pee goo*)

Spanking.

Menstruation

月经 **yuèjīng** (*yreh jing*)

Menstruation. Literally "monthly passing."

月事 **yuèshì** (*yreh shih*)

Period, menstruation. Literally "moon thing" or "monthly matters."

大姨妈 **dàyímā** (*dah ee ma*)

Auntie. A euphemism for "period."

老朋友 **lǎopéngyou** (*laow pung yo*)

Euphemism for "period." Literally "old friend." Thus, to say you're having your period you would say 我老朋友来了 **wǒ lǎopéngyou lái le** (*wuh laow pung yo lie luh*): "My old friend has arrived." Mainly used in southern China and Taiwan.

倒霉 **dǎoméi** (*dow may*)

Literally "have bad luck." A euphemism for one's period. More common in northern China.

那个 **nèigè** (*nay guh*)

Another euphemism that literally means "that." Usages include 我有那个 **wǒ yǒu nèigè** (*wuh yo nay guh*), "I have *that*," and "I've got you know what."

Miscellaneous

叫春 **jiàochūn** (*jow chren*)

Moan (in a sexual context). 叫 **jiào** (*jow*) means "yell" or "call," and 春 **chūn** (*chren*) means "love" or "life." This is also the term for a female cat howling when it's in heat.

叫床 **jiàochuáng** (*jow chwahng*)

Moan (in a sexual context). Literally "call bed" or "yell bed."

石女 shí nǚ (*shih nee*)

Frigid. Literally "stone woman." Can also refer to someone unable to have sex for congenital reasons, after a character in a famous Chinese opera, *The Peony Pavilion*, whose hymen is hard as stone.

阳萎 yángwěi (*yahng way*)

Impotent. Amusingly, this is also what Chinese sports fans yell at the opposing team during sports matches.

钟点房 zhōng diǎn fáng (*johng dyinn fahng*)

A hotel where you can rent rooms by the hour.

CHAPTER SIX

Gay Slang

In 1988 the prominent sexologist Richard Green gave a lecture at Peking Union Medical College, the top medical school in China, and was famously told by several physicians in the audience that "there are no homosexuals in China." Homosexuality had been persecuted since 1949 and throughout the Cultural Revolution, to the point of total invisibility, and at the time Green gave his lecture, just ten years after the end of that dark time, gays and lesbians in China were only beginning to emerge from underground.

The government finally began to acknowledge homosexuality in 1990, partly because it realized that it needed to engage the gay community in order to deal with the rising AIDS crisis, and since then, depending on the political atmosphere, official acceptance of gays has waxed and waned.

The late 1980s had already seen the first official media reports about isolated incidents of same-sex couples being allowed to live a married life. In 1997 "hooliganism," an umbrella term understood to include homosexual behavior (there was never any explicit law dealing with homosexuality), was dropped from the penal code. In 2000 openly gay and lesbian people appeared on TV in China for the first time, and in 2001 China officially took homosexuality off its list of mental disorders. Today you can see same-sex couples openly holding hands at the mall (at least in the biggest cities); the atmosphere in any gay club, ABBA and all, feels utterly carefree; and the lesbian sexual orientation of at least two of the biggest pop singers in China is an almost laughably open secret.

On the other hand, the movie *Brokeback Mountain* was rejected for screening in mainland China despite director Ang Lee's celebrity status in the country, gay couples from abroad are no longer allowed to adopt Chinese babies, and after the May 2008 Sichuan earthquake, gays and lesbians were among the groups barred from donating blood to help victims.

Duì shí

The ironic thing about official and social ambivalence toward gays is that China in fact has a centuries-long tradition of homosexuality, which, while sometimes lampooned, was generally at least tolerated and at times even extolled. Many scholars believe that it was the first arrival of westerners into China toward the end of the Qing dynasty, in the mid to late nineteenth century, that first introduced the idea of homosexuality as something "wrong" and an aberrant, pathological condition.

The first vague allusion to homosexuality appears in prehistoric times, during the Shang dynasty (1766–1122 BC). From there, many more, and more explicit, accounts crop up both throughout the period and during subsequent dynasties. Many emperors were known to have had male lovers, and same-sex relations between men appear in one of China's greatest literary works, *Dream of the Red Chamber*. From these, and from accounts written by westerners visiting China during the Qing dynasty, we know, among other details, that marriage between men was common in Fujian Province and that Beijing was positively crawling with male brothels.

There is less in the way of an ancient historical record about lesbian behavior, as women generally could not read or write and led extremely cloistered lives, but mentions of maids within the imperial court, or of Buddhist and Taoist nuns, sleeping with each other do surface here and there. More is known about same-sex female relationships in modern times, much of it tied up with marriage resistance movements in Guangdong and other parts of southern China during the late 1800s and early 1900s, in which women formed organized alliances and took vows never to marry—some of these women are still alive today, living as couples in homes they purchased together.

As you'll see in the next few pages, there are, in addition to the contemporary terms, many literary euphemisms for homosexuality, which were in use during ancient times. These have all been only recently revived—part of a movement within the gay Chinese community to reclaim a past from which it has been cut off for so long, and to remind us all of a time when there was nothing strange, or even noteworthy, about being gay.

Ancient euphemisms for homosexuality

There are many, many more stories like the few offered below, which during ancient times offered innumerable expressions for homosexuality via allusion to the famed persons involved or to a detail of the story. I am leaving them out, however, in favor of the most well-known and common terms in use today.

断袖余桃 **duàn xiù yú táo** (*dwun show ee taow*)

An idiomatic expression referring to homosexuality, derived from ancient Chinese literature. Literally "cut sleeve, leftover peach." See below for origins.

断袖 **dùan xiù** (*dwun show*)

Short for 断袖之癖 **dùan xiù zhī pǐ** (*dwun show jih pee*), "the passion of the cut sleeve," referring to a story about Ai, the emperor of Han (27−1 BC). The story goes that one day he had to get out of bed and, rather than wake his male lover who had fallen asleep on his sleeve, chose to cut off the sleeve of his robe. Thus any phrases involving a cut sleeve refer to homosexuality.

余桃 **yú táo** (*ee taow*)

A euphemism for homosexuality, dating to ancient times. Literally "the leftover peach," referring to a story recorded in *Han Feizi* (the writings of the philosopher Han Fei, who lived from 280–233 BC) about a beautiful male youth who picked a peach from a tree, bit into it, and found it so sweet that he offered the rest to Ling, the ruler of Wei (534–493 BC), who was touched by the gesture. Thus phrases like 分桃之爱 **fēn táo zhī ài** (*fen taow jih aye*), "love of the shared peach," or really any reference to **yú táo** or 分桃 **fēn táo** (*fen taow*), "sharing peaches," are expressions that refer to love between men.

龙阳癖 **Lóng Yáng pǐ** (*lohng yahng pee*)

Literally "the passion of Long Yang" and a euphemism for homosexuality. Lord Long Yang was a gay nobleman mentioned in the eighteenth-century classic *Dream of the Red Chamber*. According to the tale, which takes place during China's warring states period (from sometime during the fifth century BC to 221 BC), Lord Long Yang was fishing with his lover, the ruler of Wei, and suddenly burst into tears. The king asked what was wrong, upon which Long Yang said that catching bigger fish made him want to throw back the smaller ones, which surely meant that, with so many beauties in the world, some day the ruler would discard him in favor of a greater beauty. Romantically, the ruler of Wei then made a public decree that "Anyone who dares to speak of other beauties will be executed along with his entire family." To this day, **Lóng Yáng** is sometimes used to refer to a young, pretty boy in a gay relationship, and it is also the name for an international gay Asian network called the Long Yang Club.

男风 **nán fēng** (*nahn fung*) or 南风 **nán fēng** (*nahn fung*)

The former literally means "male practice" and was more or less a technical term referring to homosexuality during the Ming dynasty (1368–1644). The latter was a homophonous, and poetic, play on that word and literally means "southern custom," also connoting "southern wind." The euphemism "southern custom" was based on a common belief throughout China that homosexuality originated in, or at least was more common in, the South (mainly Fujian and Guangdong provinces). There is indeed a great deal of documentation of commonly practiced homosexual customs in those areas. For example, it was noted during the seventeenth century that it was usual for upper-class and educated men in Fujian to marry other men. An older man would buy a boy-bride from the boy's parents, a marriage ceremony was performed, and the older man's family would financially support the younger man in every way, just as in a traditional heterosexual marriage. The older man was called 契兄 **qìxiōng** (*chee shyohng*), literally "sworn older brother," and the younger one was called 契弟 **qìdì** (*chee dee*), "sworn little brother." There is documentation of some such marriages that lasted as long as twenty years, but typically they only lasted until the younger man reached the standard age for heterosexual marriage, upon which they "divorced" and the older man often paid to secure him a good female bride and otherwise helped establish him in society.

对食 **duìshí** (*dway shih*)

Literally "eat facing each other." The earliest mention of lesbianism in Chinese history was of two women from the harem of the emperor Cheng of Han, who, according to imperial records, always ate facing each other and slept to-gether.

Contemporary terms

Many Chinese simply say "gay" in English. "Gay" is usually understood to mean gay men, while lesbians mainly go by 拉拉 **lālā** (*lah lah*). Nonetheless, there are several Chinese terms for homosexuality as well:

同性恋 **tóngxìngliàn** (*tohng sheeng lyinn*)
Homosexual.

同性爱 **tóngxìng'ài** (*tohng sheeng aye*)
Gay love. Literally "same-sex love."

同志 **tóngzhì** (*tohng jih*)
Gay. Literally "comrade," the form of address used during revolutionary times and still used today by government officials and older Chinese. First adopted in 1987 by gay rights activists in Hong Kong.

女同志 **nǚ tóngzhì** (*nee tohng jih*)
Lesbian. Literally "female comrade."

大同 **dàtóng** (*dah tohng*)
A relatively new term coined by university students, short for 大学生同志 **dàxuéshēng tóngzhì** (*dah shreh shung tohng jih*), which means "gay university students."

断背 **duànbèi** (*dwun bay*)

Literally "brokeback," after Ang Lee's movie *Brokeback Mountain*. A euphemism for homosexuality.

líng hào

yī hào

Duàn bèi

玻璃 **bōlí** (*bwuh lee*)

A euphemism for "gay." Literally "crystal" or "glass." Not often used in speech, but known by most gay Chinese people. It comes from the seminal 1980 novel *Crystal Boys*, by the gay Taiwanese writer Pai Hsien-Yung. The novel's mention of "crystal boys" is itself a reference to a passage from the classic work *Dream of the Red Chamber*.

拉拉 **lālā** (*lah lah*) or 拉子 **lāzi** (*lah dz*)

The most commonly used word for "lesbian." **Lāzi** is used in Taiwan and was coined (based on the sound of the English "lesbian" or "lez") by a lesbian Taiwanese writer named 邱妙津 **Qiu Miaojin** (*chyoe myow gene*). When the term spread to the mainland it became **lālā** instead.

T & P

Terms for lesbian roles. The *T* stands for "tomboy" and the *P* refers to 老婆 **lǎopó** (*laow pwuh*), or "wife" in Chinese. The terms are equivalent to "butch" and "femme" in English.

娘 T **niáng T** (*nyahng T*)

Girly T, soft butch. A lesbian who identifies as a T but is still a bit feminine or girly.

爷 P **yé P** (*yeh P*)

Grandfather P. A lesbian who identifies as a P but is a bit manly.

不分 **bù fēn** (*boo fen*)

Literally "don't differentiate." Means that you don't particularly identify as a T or P, and that you also have no preference in terms of which type you're into.

帅 T 美 P **shuài T měi P** (*shwhy T may P*)

帅 T **Shuài T** (*shwhy T*) means "handsome tomboy(s)" and 美 P **měi P** (*may P*) is "pretty wife" or "pretty wives." You might use them together to say something like "This club is full of handsome tomboys and pretty wives tonight!"

TT 恋 **TT liàn** (*TT lyinn*)

Tomboy-tomboy love, when two tomboys date.

T 吧 **T ba** (*T bah*)

A lesbian bar just for tomboys. Since most Chinese lesbians believe that a T and a P should date each other, the exact reason for the existence of a tomboy-only bar is somewhat mystifying.

自梳女 **zì shū nǚ** (*dz shoe nee*)

Comb sisters (literally "a woman who combs her hair by herself"). Referring to a group of women in Guangdong and other parts of southern China during the late 1800s and early 1900s who vowed to resist the oppressions of the Confucian conception of marriage. While **zì shū nǚ** were not necessarily all lesbians, they are perceived in popular culture as some sort of lesbian cult and have also been embraced as such by the Chinese lesbian community.

主动 **zhǔdòng** (*joo dohng*)

Top, giver, pitcher, husband. Literally "active."

被动 **bèidòng** (*bay dohng*)

Bottom, taker, catcher, wife. Literally "passive."

1 号 **yī hào** (*ee how*) or just 1 **yī** (*ee*)

Literally "number one" or just "one." Means "top," "pitcher," or "husband" because the number one looks like a penis.

0 号 **líng hào** (*ling how*) or just 0 **líng** (*ling*)

Literally "number zero" or just "zero." Means "bottom," "catcher," or "wife" because a "one" can be inserted into a "zero." You might hear two guys flirting at a bar ask, "你是 1 还是 0?" "**Nǐ shì yī hái shì líng?**": "Are you a one or a zero?"

0.5 **líng diǎn wǔ** (*ling dyinn oo*)

Either, versatile. That is, you can be either the 1 or the 0. You can also indicate that you're a 0.5 by saying 全能 **quán néng** (*chren nung*), which means "all can"; that is, "can do all."

Rice queen

A gay guy who prefers Asian men (this would simply be said in English, as there is no translation in Chinese).

Potato queen

A gay guy who prefers white men (this would simply be said in English, as there is no translation in Chinese).

MB

For "money boy" (and said in English). A (usually young) man who takes money for sex with other men.

T 少 **T shào** (*T shaow*)

A woman who takes money for sex with other women.

哥哥 **gēge** (*guh guh*)

A manly gay man. Literally "older brother." Can also imply sugar daddy.

弟弟 **dìdi** (*dee dee*)

A girly, or effeminate, gay man. Literally "younger brother." Can also imply a person being supported by a sugar daddy.

熊 **xióng** (*shyohng*)

Literally "bear." Taken directly from the English slang for a gay man with a bigger, slightly chubby build.

人妖 **rényāo** (*ren yow*)

Lady-boy.

反串 **fǎnchuàn** (*fahn chwun*)

Drag queen (applies both to men who dress up as women and to women who dress up as men in performances).

CC or just C

Queen (and said in English). Used because CC sounds like "sissy" to Chinese ears. Many Chinese gays also just say "sissy" in English for a queen or a feminine guy.

鞋号 **xié hào** (*shyih how*)

Literally "shoe size." Used online to imply penis size.

炮友 **pàoyǒu** (*pow yo*)

Fuck buddy. 炮 **Pào** (*pow*) means "cannon" and is a euphemism for ejaculation, while 友 **yǒu** (*yo*) means friends.

Gay 吧 **"Gay" ba** (*gay bah*)

Gay café.

公司 **gōngsī** (*gohng sih*)

Taiwan slang for a park where gay men gather and meet. Literally "company" but shares the same initial syllable with "park," which is 公园 **gōngyuán** (*gohng yren*). One particularly well-known "company" is the 2/28 Peace Memorial Park in Taipei.

双性恋 **shuāngxìngliàn** (*shwahng sheeng lyinn*)

Bisexuality. Literally "love for both sexes."

阴阳人 **yīnyáng rén** (*een yahng ren*)

Transsexual or hermaphrodite. Literally "yin-yang person." May also be used insultingly to refer to an extremely manly woman or to an extremely effeminate man.

同仁女 **tóngrén nǚ** (*tohng ren nee*)

Fag hag. 同仁 **Tóng rén** (*tohng ren*) means "colleagues," but 同 **tóng** (*tohng*) also alludes to gay men, while 女 **nǚ** (*nee*) means "woman," so the overall suggestion is a woman who has close associations with gay men.

同志牛皮糖 **tóngzhì niúpí tang** (*tohng jih nyoo pee tahng*)

Fag hag. Literally "gay leather-candy." 同志 **Tóngzhì** (*tohng jih*) means "gay," and 牛皮糖 **niúpí tang** (*nyoo pee tahng*) is a type of sticky candy, thus suggesting sticking to gay guys.

出柜 **chū guì** (*choo gway*)

Come out of the closet.

异性恋 **yìxìngliàn** (*ee sheeng lyinn*)

Heterosexuality. Literally "love for the opposite sex."

直人 **zhírén** (*jih ren*)

Straight. Literally "straight person."

CHAPTER SEVEN

Behaving Badly

In the last few decades leading up to the 1949 Communist revolution, the city of Shanghai was unquestionably the most sinful place on earth. "If God lets Shanghai endure, he owes an apology to Sodom and Gomorrah," said one missionary living there in the early twenties.

The Whore of Asia, as the city was known, was born in 1842 at the conclusion of the Opium War, when the British forced imperial China to open the port city to foreign trade, and the British—soon followed by the Americans, the French, and numerous other nationalities—quickly established settlements there, each governed by its own rule of law. The mishmash of completely different governments, laws, and courts meant that evading arrest was as simple as walking a block in one direction or another (or buying a fake passport for some random nationality). That, the extreme contrasts of fabulous wealth and decrepit poverty, the opium business driving all the city's moneymaking, the political turmoil brought about by the overthrow of imperial rule, and an ensuing period during which various parts of China were ruled by a rotating cast of brutally violent warlords—not to mention numerous other causes—all combined to make Shanghai the final destination for hedonists, capitalists, adventurers, journalists, businessmen, prostitutes, gangsters, political refugees, gun runners, intellectuals, arms dealers, movie stars, and dilettantes from every corner of the globe.

Decadence reached its apex in the 1930s, when the opium trade had grown into a full-fledged international drug cartel trafficking in morphine, heroin, and cocaine. The cargo made its way into Europe, South America, and the United States—all controlled by a Chinese mob boss who was simultaneously head of the Nationalist government's Opium Suppression Bureau. The city had three hundred jazz cabarets and a hundred thousand prostitutes, organized gambling thrived on the largest scale of any city in the world, in addition to opium parlors and gambling halls there were nightclubs that featured erotic shows with real live onstage sex, and at some hotels you could order heroin via room service.

Today Shanghai is still known for its nightlife but compared to its heyday is a relatively staid financial city. The influx of foreigners coming to misbehave, however, continues, alive and well, throughout the country. For most, this seems to involve drinking oneself into oblivion every night, doing a lot of drugs, and sleeping around with the locals while teaching English and "finding yourself."

Whether your vice of choice is methamphetamines or auto theft, hookers galore or simply partying till dawn, here is the necessary vocabulary for every naughty deed under the Eastern sun.

Fun and partying

玩 **wán** (*wahn*)

Play. A generic word for going out, partying, or any kind of social activity.

外出 **wài chū** (*why choo*)

Going out.

酒吧 **jǐubā** (*joe bah*)

Bar.

夜总会 **yèzǒnghuì** (*yeh dzohng hway*)

Club. Literally "night meeting."

迪厅 **dītīng** (*dee teeng*)

Club. Literally "disco hall."

夜店 **yèdiàn** (*yeh dyinn*)

Nightclub. The term encompasses discos, karaoke bars, cafés, and video arcades and can also refer to establishments offering illegal sex services. The term originated in Taiwan and has spread through southern China. It's used to a lesser degree by young people in northern China as well.

迪斯科 **dīsīkē** (*dee suh kuh*)

Disco. A transliteration of the English.

轰趴 **hōngpā** (*hohng pah*)

A transliteration based on the English phrase "house party" but with the additional connotation of having so much fun that you collapse: 轰 **hōng** (*hohng*) means "an explosion" and

趴 **pā** (*pah*) means "lie on your stomach," so the words together suggest something along the lines of being struck dead. Used in Taiwan.

蹦迪 **bèngdī** (*bung dee*)

Disco dance.

卡拉 OK **kǎ lā OK** (*kah lah OK*) or KTV

Both terms mean "karaoke." The first is a transliteration of the English word, but most Chinese simply say KTV, pronouncing the letters as you would in English.

麦霸 **màibà** (*my bah*)

Microphone monopolist. 麦 **Mài** (*my*) refers to a mike and 霸 **bà** (*bah*) means "tyrant." A term popular among young people to describe someone who hogs the mike at karaoke.

刷夜 **shuā yè** (*shwah yeh*)

To stay out all night, hang out with shady people, run with a bad crowd. Literally "swap night."

Alcohol

喝酒 **hē jǐu** (*huh joe*)

To drink alcohol.

喝多 **hēduō** (*huh dwuh*)

Drunk, hung over. Literally "drink much."

喝醉 **hēzuì** (*huh dzway*)

Wasted. Literally "drink tipsy."

喝大了 **hē dà le** (*huh dah luh*)

A northern Chinese way to say "very drunk" or "wasted." Literally "drank big."

干 **gān** (*gahn*) or 干了 **gān le** (*gahn luh*)

Drain one's glass, shoot it, suck down a drink really fast. Literally "dry [the glass]."

酒滥用 **jǐu lànyòng** (*joe lahn yohng*)

Alcohol abuse. Literally "alcohol excessive use."

酒鬼 **jǐuguǐ** (*joe gway*)

Alcoholic. Literally "alcohol ghost."

白酒 **báijǐu** (*buy joe*)

Chinese liquor. Literally "white alcohol." **Báijǐu** is notoriously strong (about the same proof as vodka) and even more notoriously foul tasting. It is drunk only in shots, accompanied by an elaborate set of rituals and social mores that, in a nutshell, enable Chinese men to bully each other into puking oblivion beneath a veneer of politeness.

醉酒驾驶 **zuì jǐu jià shǐ** (*dzway joe jah shih*)

Drink and drive.

Mild vices

撒谎 **sāhuǎng** (sah hwahng)

Tell a lie. Literally "release yellow."

荤的 **hūn de** (*hwen duh*)

Dirty, obscene, pornographic. Literally "meat or fish," referring to Buddhism, which considers such foods unclean or dirty. One term that uses this is 荤段子 **hūn duànzǐ** (*hwen swun dz*), meaning "dirty joke."

吃枪药 **chī qiāng yào** (*chih chyahng yow*)

To speak rudely or insolently. Literally "to swallow gunpowder." As in: "Why are you being such an asshole—did you swallow gunpowder?"

喷粪 **pēn fèn** (*pen fen*)

To swear, curse, say dirty words. Literally "spurt manure" or "puff out dung."

毛腔 **máoqiāng** (*maow chyahng*)

Swear, curse, lose one's temper. Literally "hairy chests."

嘴臭 **zuǐ chòu** (*dzway choe*)

Literally "stinky mouth." Refers to someone who is vulgar or rude or swears a lot.

裸奔 **luǒ bēn** (*lwuh ben*)

Streaking.

玩心跳 **wán xīntiào** (*wahn sheen tyow*)

Thrill seeking. Literally "play with your heartbeat." That is, to engage in activities that will quicken your heartbeat.

飙车 **biāo chē** (*byow chuh*)

Drag racing. Literally "whirlwind car."

钢管舞 **gāng guǎn wǔ** (*gahng gwahn oo*)

Pole dancing. This activity has become popular among some urban Chinese women as a form of exercise, with at least a few of them unaware that westerners associate it with stripping.

脱衣女郎 **tuōyī nǚláng** (*twuh ee duh nee lahng*)

Stripper. Literally "taking-off-clothes girl."

路怒 **lù nù** (*loo noo*)

Road rage. Traffic in Beijing, and China's other major cities, is notoriously bad.

欺骗 **qīpiàn** (*chee pyinn*)

Cheat (any kind of cheating). A cheater is a 骗子 **piànzi** (*pyinn dz*).

小混混 **xiǎo húnhún** (*shyaow hwen hwen*) or 混子 **hunzǐ** (*hwen dz*)

Small-time crook.

假活儿 **jiǎ huór** (*jah hwurr*)

Beijing slang for a swindler or con man. Literally "fake work."

小报告 **xiǎobào gào** (*shaow baow gaow*—all three syllables rhyme with "cow")

Snitching. Literally "file little secret reports."

踩 **cǎi** (*tsigh*)

To slander, libel, insult. Literally "step on."

暴打 **bào dǎ** (*baow dah*)

Beat up.

满地找牙 **mǎn dì zhǎo yá** (*mahn dee jaow yah*)

Get beaten up. Literally "find [one's] teeth on the ground." Used in northern China.

掐 **qiā** (*chyah*) or 掐架 **qiājià** (*chyah jah*)

Fight.

干 **gān** (*gahn*) or 干架 **gānjià** (*gahn jah*)

Fight. Also slang for "kill."

废 **fèi** (*fay*)

To injure or maim. Can also mean "to break" or "amputate."

给他个颜色看看 **gěi tā ge yánsè kànkan** (*gay tah guh yen suh kahn kahn*)

Beat him up. Literally "give him a color to see" (that color being red).

找不着北 **zhǎobùzháoběi** (*jow boo jow bay*)

Knock out, beat up. Can also mean "to get confused." Literally "unable to find where north is."

五指山红 **wǔ zhǐ shān hóng** (*ooh jih shahn hohng*)

Literally "five fingers turning red." That is, a slap so hard it leaves five red finger marks on your face.

全武行 **quán wǔ xíng** (*chren oo sheeng*)

Fighting in public. The term originally referred to acrobatic fighting in Chinese opera performances. Now it also refers to fighting in the streets or other public places.

铁头功 **tiě tóu gōng** (*tyih toe gohng*)

Head butt.

打一拳 **dǎ yī quán** (dah ee chren)

Punch. Literally "hit (with) a fist." Or you can specify the person being punched by saying 给他一拳 **gěi tā yī quán** (*gay tah ee chren*), literally "give him a fist," meaning "punch him."

顺出去 **shùn chūqù** (*shwen choo chee*)

Means "to carry something out vertically," for example, turning a dresser on its side and moving it out of the bedroom, but can also mean carrying a person out after beating them up, as when someone is being kicked out of a bar. Used in northern China only.

脚底摸油 **jiǎo dǐ mō yóu** (*jyow dee mwuh yo*)

Cut and run, leave the scene of the crime, remove oneself from an awkward situation. Literally "apply oil to the soles of your feet"; that is, to speed your retreat.

Pornography

黄 **huáng** (*hwahng*) or 黄色 **huángsè** (*hwahng suh*)

Obscene, dirty, pornographic. Literally "yellow." In Chinese
class you're most likely to learn 色情 **sèqíng** (*suh cheeng*) for
"pornography"; it, however, is considered outdated. Nowadays anything pornographic or dirty is referred to as "yellow," an association that may have originated in the
nineteenth century, when French novels, recognizable by
their yellow covers, became notorious throughout the world
for their "immoral" sexual content. Thus a pornographic
movie is a 黄色电影 **huángsè diànyǐng** (*hwahng suh dyinn
ing*), literally "yellow movie"; a 黄带 **huángdài** (*hwahng die*),
"yellow tape"; or 黄片 **huángpiān** (*hwahng pyinn*), literally
"yellow piece." A porno mag is a 黄色书刊 **huángsè shūkān**
(*hwahng suh shoo kahn*), literally "yellow book," and a dirty
joke or story is a 黄段子 **huáng duànzǐ** (*hwahng dwun dz*), or
"yellow episode."

毛片 **máopiān** (*mao pyinn*)

Porn video. Literally "hair tape" because you can see pubic
hair.

A 片 **A piàn** (*A pyinn*)

Hard-core porn movie. Literally "A video," for "adult video"
(though, interestingly, some Chinese mistakenly believe the
A stands for American).

三级片 **sānjí piàn** (*sahn gee pyinn*)

Soft-core porn movie. Literally "level-three video," referring
to the most restrictive level in Hong Kong's movie-rating
system.

Drugs

吸毒 **xīdú** (*she do*)

To take drugs. Literally "suck poison."

毒贩子 **dúfànzǐ** (*do fahn dz*) or just 毒贩 **dúfàn** (*do fahn*)

Drug dealer. "To deal drugs" is 贩毒 **fàndú** (*fahn do*).

药物滥用 **yàowù lànyòng** (*yaow oo lahn yohng*) or 毒品滥用
dúpǐn lànyòng (*do peen lahn yohng*)

Substance abuse. Literally "drug excessive use." The first
term can mean any type of drugs, including medicine, and
the second term specifically means illegal drugs, but both are
frequently used. You can insert the name of a drug in front
of 滥用 **lànyòng** to indicate abuse of that specific drug.

瘾君子 **yǐnjūnzǐ** (*een jwen dz*)

Drug addict. Literally "addicted gentleman" or "addicted
nobleperson," because once upon a time only wealthy people
could afford drugs, and opium was considered a status symbol.

抽 **chōu** (*choe*)

Smoke (as in smoking marijuana, opium, heroin, etc.). 吸 **Xī**
(*she*), literally "inhale," can be used too, though it is less
common than **chōu**.

用 **yòng** (*yohng*)

Use. Can be inserted in front of any drug name to indicate
use of that drug. For heroin or opium, however, it's more
common to say **yòng** than **xī** or **chōu** (above), even though
they can be smoked.

逗 **dòu** (*doe*)

Use. Has a variety of unrelated literal meanings, including "stop" and "tease," but is also used as slang for using drugs.

飞 **fēi** (*fay*)

High. Literally "to fly." Usually describes being high on marijuana but can also be used for ecstasy, heroin, and other euphoric drugs. 飞起 **Fēi qǐ** (*fay chee*), literally "flying upwards," describes the feeling of getting high, and 太起了 **tài qǐ le** (*tie chee luh*), literally "rising too much," describes being too high.

大 **dà** (*dah*) or 大了 **dà le** (*dah luh*)

An all-purpose Beijing word for "drunk," "wasted," "high," "fucked up," etc.. Literally "big." Can indicate being under the influence of any drug. You can simply say, "我大了" "**Wǒ dà le**" (*wuh dah luh*), literally "I'm big," to mean "I'm high" or "I'm on something" or "I'm fucked up." Or you can be more specific by inserting various drug-related verbs (smoke, use, eat) in front; for example 我抽大了 **wǒ chōu dà le** (*wuh choe dah luh*) literally means "I smoked big" and indicates that you are high on marijuana or something else that can be smoked.

有感觉 **yǒu gǎnjué** (*yo gahn dreh*)

Literally "have a feeling" or, rather, "I feel something" or "I'm feeling it," indicating that you're feeling the effects of a drug, whether you're feeling high or a trip is setting in or things are starting to get funny or whatever.

沉了 **chén le** (*chen luh*) or 颓了 **tuí le** (*tway luh*)

Literally "drop" and "decline," respectively. Both can describe dropping, crashing, or a comedown.

大麻 **dàmá** (*dah ma*)

Marijuana, hashish.

呼 **hū** (*who*)

Smoke (as in weed or hash). Literally "exhale." More common in northern China. Southerners tend to say **chōu** (page 150).

咳 **hāi** (*high*)

High (on marijuana). Literally, this is the onomatopoeic word for "sigh," but it is used to mean "high" since it sounds just like the English word.

可乐 **kělè** (*kuh luh*)

Coke. Slang for cocaine (and also the Chinese brand name for Coca-Cola). The formal words for cocaine are 古柯碱 **gǔkējiǎn** (*goo kuh jinn*), the scientific name more often used in Taiwan and Hong Kong, and 可卡因 **kěkǎyīn** (*kuh ka een*), a transliteration of the English.

吸 **xī** (*she*)

Snort. Literally "suck in."

道 **dào** (*dow*)

Line (in connection with coke use). Literally "road" or "path." "A line of coke" is 一道可乐 **yī dào kělè** (*ee daow kuh luh*).

摇头丸 **yáotóuwán** (*yow toe wahn*)

Ecstasy (official name). Literally "shake-head pill." Unlike the English term, no user would ever use this full name to refer to the drug. Most people either say "E" or one of the two slang terms below.

药 **yào** (*yow*)

Pill (slang for an ecstasy pill). Literally "medicine" or "drug." Doing or swallowing a pill is 吃药 **chī yào** (*chih yow*), literally "eat medicine." There is no direct Chinese equivalent to "rolling" to describe being on the drug, but you can instead use some of the words mentioned earlier, such as **fēi** or **dà le**.

丸仔 **wánzǎi** (*wahn dzigh*)

Southern Chinese slang for ecstasy. Northerners usually just say "E," though 药 **yào** (*yow*) is common too.

开他敏 **kāitāmǐn** (*kigh tah meen*)

Ketamine. A transliteration of the English. As in many other countries, Special K is fast usurping ecstasy as a popular club drug in China. This is exacerbated by the fact that several factories within its borders produce ketamine for legitimate veterinary use, and thus the drug is cheaper in China.

K 粉 **K fěn** (*K fen*) or, more commonly, just K

Slang for ketamine. The first term literally means "K powder."

麻黄碱 **máhuángjiǎn** (*mah hwahng jinn*)

Ephedrine. Widely available and abused in China because ephedra, the plant from which ephedrine is derived, is native to southern China (and used in traditional Chinese medicine), and the production and export of the drug is a massive industry.

冰 **bīng** (*bing*)

Ice (slang for crystal methamphetamine). Ice use is growing by leaps and bounds in China, for the reasons discussed in the previous entry (ephedrine is a precursor chemical for methamphetamine).

溜冰 **liūbīng** (*lyew bing*)

Doing ice. Literally "ice skating."

致幻剂 **zhìhuànjì** (*jih hwun gee*)

Hallucinogen. 致幻 **Zhìhuàn** means "hallucination" or "hallucinate."

有幻觉 **yǒuhuànjué** (*yo hwun jreh*)

Hallucinate. Literally "have a hallucination."

蘑菇 **mógū** (*mwuh goo*)

Mushrooms. There isn't any direct equivalent to "trip" or "tripping" in Chinese, but you can use some of the words mentioned at the beginning of the drug section, like **fēi** or **dà le**.

L

Slang for LSD. Pronounced like the English letter. The verb for doing LSD is 贴 **tiē** (*tyih*), literally "to stick" or "affix."

邮票 **yóupiào** (*yo pyow*)

Slang for LSD. Literally "postage stamp."

镇静剂 **zhènjìngjì** (*jen jing gee*)

Tranquilizer or depressants. Literally "calm drug."

笑气 **xiàoqì** (*shyow chee*)

Laughing gas.

止疼药 **zhǐténgyào** (*jhh tung yow*) or 止疼片 **zhǐténgpiàn** (*jhh tung pyinn*)

Painkillers.

麻醉药 **mázuìyào** (*mah dzway yow*)

Narcotics.

吗啡 **mǎfēi** (*ma fay*)

Morphine. A transliteration of the English.

美沙酮 **měishātóng** (*may shah tohng*) or 美沙粉 **měishāfěn** (*may shah fen*)

Methadone. A transliteration of the English.

可待因 **kědàiyīn** (*kuh die een*).

Codeine. A transliteration of the English.

神仙水 **shénxiānshuǐ** (*shen shin shway*)

Slang for codeine. Literally "celestial water."

海洛因 **hǎiluòyīn** (*high lwuh een*)

Heroin. A transliteration of the English. Heroin is by far the most abused drug in China. The country borders the world's top opium-producing countries (the Golden Triangle of Myanmar, Laos, Vietnam, and Thailand; as well as Afghanistan and Pakistan), making it an important transit route for trafficking of the drug. Moreover, poppy fields are also cultivated in some of China's most rural provinces. Ironically, heroin first took hold in China during the 1920s because it was considered a cure for the widespread problem of opium addiction.

粉儿 **fěnr** (*fenr*)

Northern Chinese slang for (powder) heroin. Literally "powder." The verb for doing it is 吸 **xī** (*she*), "suck in."

欣快 **xīnkuài** (*sheen kwhy*)

Euphoria. Literally "happy fast."

俚]追龙 **zhuī long** (*jway lohng*)

Literally "chasing the dragon." Refers to smoking heroin. Used in Hong Kong only.

安眠药 **ānmiányào** (*ahn myinn yow*)

Opiates. Literally "sleepy medicine."

鸦片 **yāpiàn** (*yah pyinn*)

Opium. A transliteration of the English. Opium, which was more or less forced on the Chinese by Britain during the late 1800s to deal with a trade imbalance caused by sky-high demand for Chinese porcelain and tea, has been an extraordinarily widespread problem for the country. The 1949 Communist revolution wiped out the drug almost completely, but inevitably, given that the drug is largely produced in countries that border China, it has, since the late 1980s, begun to spread once again.

安定 **āndìng** (*ahn ding*)

Diazepam (most commonly marketed as Valium). Literally "calm" or "stable."

苯环利定 **běnhuánlìdìng** (*ben hwun lee ding*)

Phencyclidine (PCP).

天使粉 **tiānshǐfěn** (*tyinn shih fen*)

Angel dust. Slang for PCP (phencyclidine).

强奸药丸 **qiángjiān yàowán** (*chyahng jin yow wahn*)

Roofies. Literally "rape pill."

FM2

Roofies. Pronounced like the English.

十字架 **shízìjià** (*shih dz jah*)

Roofies. Literally "cross" because of the cross shape that is sometimes scored into Rohypnol pills. It's more common to simply say FM2 in English, however.

类固醇 **lèigùchún** (*lay goo chwen*)

Steroids.

戒毒 **jièdú** (*jyih do*)

Kick the habit, rehabilitate, quit taking drugs. Literally "get rid of drugs."

Prostitution

Chinese police use seven classifications for prostitution. From highest to lowest, they are:

1. 包二奶 **bāoèrnǎi** (*bow er nigh*—**bāo** rhymes with "cow")

     Long ago, when Chinese men had multiple wives, 奶 **èrnǎi** (*er nigh*) referred to the second wife. Today it refers to mistresses of wealthy men and government officials, an extremely common fact of life in China: literally "packaged second-wife." A related term is:

     二奶专家 **èrnǎi zhuānjiā** (*er nigh jwahn jah*)

     Rich Chinese businessmen and government officials who collect "second wives." Literally "mistress expert."

2. 包婆 **bāopó** (*baow pwuh*—**bāo** rhymes with "cow")

     Literally "packaged wife." Women who receive payment for accompanying wealthy men or government officials on business trips or for some other fixed period of time.

3. 三厅 **sāntīng** (*sahn ting*)

     Literally "three halls." Refers to prostitution in specific venues, such as bars, clubs, karaoke parlors, teahouses, bathhouses, etc. They generally make money from tips and from a cut of the venue's "service charges." Some related terms are:

三陪小姐 **sānpéi xiǎojiě** (*sahn pay shaow jyih*)

Literally "young ladies of the three accompaniments." A common euphemism for **sāntīng** sex workers. The three accompaniments are supposedly drinking, dancing, and chatting or singing with their clients (often while being groped). Of course, the unspoken fourth accompaniment costs extra.

小姐 **xiǎojiě** (*shaow jyih*)

Whore, prostitute. Literally "little miss." **Xiǎojiě** is also an everyday form of address for waitresses, shopgirls, and any service staff in Taiwan and southern China, but due to the association with prostitution, northern Chinese instead address such personnel by the impersonal term 服务员 **fúwùyuán** (*foo oo yren*), literally "service person."

KTV 小姐 **KTV xiǎojiě** ("KTV" *shaow jyih*)

Prostitute in a karaoke parlor. Literally "karaoke miss."

吧女 **bānǔ** (*bah nee*)

Bar girl.

洗浴中心 **xǐyù zhōngxīn** (*she yee johng sheen*)

Bathhouse.

4. 叮咚小姐 **dīngdōng xiǎojie** (*deeng dohng shaow jyih*)

Literally "ding-dong girls" or "doorbell ladies." Prostitutes who solicit clients by phone in hotel rooms. If you ever stay in a Chinese hotel and get a mysterious call in the middle of the night, chances are it's a ding-dong girl.

5. 发廊妹 **fàláng mèi** (*fah lahng may*)

Prostitutes who work under the guise of a hair salon, beauty parlor, bathhouse, or massage parlor. Literally "hair salon sister." The most common services offered are hand jobs and oral sex. If you're ever looking for an actual haircut in China, look for a salon that has female customers and where the hairdressers actually appear to know how to use a pair of scissors—and even then you might very well *still* wind up getting a whispered proposition. A related term is:

按摩女 **ànmó nǚ** (*ahn mwuh nee*)

Literally "massage girl." Includes both actual masseuses who do a little extra for an additional fee and full-on prostitutes who work under the guise of being masseuses but have no idea how to give a massage.

6. 街女 **jiēnǚ** (*jyih nee*)

Literally "street girls." Prostitutes who solicit clients on the street.

7. 下工棚 **xiàgōngpéng** (*shah gohng pung*)

Literally "lower work shack." Prostitutes whose clients are migrant workers—usually men from the countryside who have found temporary work doing manual labor in the big city.

Beyond these seven official tiers, here are other words related to prostitution:

妓女 **jìnǚ** (*gee knee*)

The most neutral, formal word for prostitute.

娼妓 **chāngjì** (*chahng gee*)

Another formal term for prostitute.

鸡 **jī** (*gee*) and 野鸡 **yějī** (*yeh gee*)

Whore, prostitute, hooker. Literally "chicken" or "wild chicken/pheasant." Probably came about in Shanghai during the late 1800s and early 1900s because the city saw a sudden influx of streetwalkers, which was a relatively new sight (as opposed to women who hosted men in teahouses and brothels), and the women were said to look like chickens walking around on the street. Also a play on words because the 鸡 **jī**, meaning "chicken," sounds nearly the same as 妓 **jì** in the formal term for "prostitute" (above). A **yějī** can also be an illegal business.

站街的 **zhàn jiē de** (*jahn jyih duh*)

Streetwalker. Literally "one who stands on the street."

鸡院 **jīyuàn** (*gee yren*)

Slang term for a brothel. Literally "chicken yard."

鸭 **yā** (*yah*) or 鸭子 **yāzi** (*yah dz*)
Male prostitute. Literally "duck."

卖豆腐 **mài dòufu** (*my doe foo*)
Literally "sell tofu" and a euphemism for prostitution.

女士酒吧 **nǚshì jǐubā** (*nee shih joe bah*)
Lady bar.

皮条 **pítiáo** (*pee tyow*)
Pimp.

拉皮条 **lāpítiáo** (*lah pee tyow*)
Pimp. Literally "pull/drag prostitutes."

婊子 **biǎozi** (*byow dz*)
Whore, prostitute, hooker. Also an insult similar to "bitch."

应召女郎 **yìng zhào nǚláng** (*yeeng dzow nee lahng*)
Prostitute. Literally "call girl."

嫖 **piáo** (*pyow*) or 嫖娼 **piáochāng** (*pyow chahng*)
Visit prostitutes, whore around, pay for sex.

陪客 **péikè** (*pay kuh*)
To entertain clients—either in a legitimate business sense or in the euphemistic sense.

嫖客 **piáokè** (*pyow kuh*)

Whoremonger, john, brothel customer. Literally "whoring guest."

红灯区 **hóngdēngqū** (*hohng dung chee*)

"Red-light district." Used only in southern China and Taiwan.

出台 **chūtái** (*choo tie*)

To take home (a prostitute). A verb used when a john takes a prostitute away from the establishment and to a home or hotel instead. Literally "leave the counter."

打包 **dǎbāo** (*da baow*)

Literally the term used for a doggie bag or wrapping up leftover food to take home from a restaurant, but it can also be jokingly used to indicate that you want to take a prostitute off premises.

性病 **xìngbìng** (*sheeng bing*)

STD (sexually transmitted disease). Literally "sex disease."

花柳 **huāliǔ** (*hwah lew—lew* rhymes with "pew") / 花柳病 **huāliǔbìng** (*hwah lyew bing*)

STD. Literally "flower willow" or "flower willow disease." Flowers and willows have been used as metaphors for women since ancient times, and STDs are generally considered a disease that men get from prostitutes.

脏病 **zāngbìng** (*jahng bing*)
STD. Literally "dirty disease."

Sexual perversion

色鬼 **sèguǐ** (*suh gway*)
Sex maniac. Literally "sex ghost."

色情狂 **sèqíngkuáng** (*suh cheeng kwahng*)
Sex maniac. Literally "sex crazy person."

流氓 **liúmáng** (*lyew mahng*)
A derogatory term for a man that may mean he is just generally "bad" or "rowdy" or a "hooligan" but may also indicate sexual perversion involving women. Women frequently use this word in reference to a man who is aggressively hitting on them.

狼 **láng** (*lahng*)
Dirty guy. Literally "wolf."

色狼 **sèláng** (*suh lahng*)
Literally "colored wolf." A lecherous man. Like **liúmáng** (above), women often use this to describe men who are aggressively hitting on them. Originally it referred exclusively to older men who prey on younger women, but now it refers to men of any age.

色迷迷的 **sèmīmīdè** (*suh me me duh*)

Lecherous. Literally "colored fantasy." A lecherous man, synonymous with **liúmáng** or **sèláng** (above), is a 色迷迷的男人 **sèmīmīdè nánrén** (*suh me me duh nahn ren*), and you would say that he has 色迷迷的眼神 **sèmīmīdè yǎnshén** (*suh me me duh yen shen*), or "sex in his eyes," literally "colored eyes."

下流 **xiàliú** (*shah lew*)

Perverted. Literally "below flowing."

调戏 **tiáoxì** (*tyow she*)

To take advantage of or harass a woman. Most often used to refer to a man verbally assaulting a woman with obscene words.

花老头 **huā lǎotóu** (*hwa laow toe*)

Dirty old man.

咸猪手 **xiánzhūshǒu** (*shin joo show*)

Groping. Used in Taiwan and Guangdong Province. Literally "salty pig hands." In Taiwan and Guangdong, a man who pays unwanted sexual attention to a woman (groping, etc.) is called a 猪哥 **zhūgē** (*joo guh*), literally "pig brother."

暴露狂 **bàolù kuáng** (*baow loo kwahng*)

Flash, flashing. Literally "showing crazy person."

恶趣味 **è qùwèi** (*uh chee way*)

Literally "repulsive interests." Originating in Japan, the term refers to five types of sexual perversion: (1) interest in young girls, (2) homosexuality, (3) bondage and sadomasochism, (4) Freudian issues—for example an Oedipus complex—and (5) incest.

乱伦 **luànlún** (*lwun lwen*)

Incest. Literally "messy logical sequence."

希腊剧 **xīlàjù** (*she la jee*)

Incest. Literally "Greek play."

性骚扰 **xìngsāorǎo** (*sheeng saow raow*)

Sexual assault, molestation. Literally "sex interrupts."

怪叔叔 **guài shūshu** (*gwhy shoo shoo*)
Pedophile. Literally "weird uncle." Used in Taiwan.

强奸 **qiángjiān** (*chyahng gin*)
Rape. Literally "forced sex."

Crime

罪犯 **zuìfàn** (*dzway fahn*)
Criminal.

拎包党 **līn bāo dǎng** (*leen baow dahng*)
Purse snatcher.

三只手 **sān zhī shǒu** (*sahn jih show*)
Pickpocket. Literally "three hands."

小偷 **xiǎotōu** (*shyaow toe*)
Thief. Literally "little steal."

顺 **shùn** (*shwen*) or 顺走 **shùn zǒu** (*shwen dzoe*)
Beijing slang for "steal." Literally "smooth" and "smoothly walk away," respectively.

纵火 **zònghuǒ** (*dzohng hwuh*)
Arson. Literally "start fire."

走私 **zǒusī** (*dzoe sih*)
Smuggling. Literally "go private."

黄牛 **huángníu** (*hwahng nyoo*)

Literally "yellow ox." A ticket scalper or someone who buys and sells foreign currency on the black market—the sight of a mob of people trying to get tickets resembles a herd of cows. Can also mean a person who doesn't repay debts. Originated in Shanghai but now used everywhere.

洗钱 **xǐqián** (*she chin*)

Money laundering.

敲诈 **qiāozhà** (*chyow jah*)

Blackmail. Literally "knock cheat."

行贿 **xínghuì** (*sheeng hway*)

Bribery.

封口费 **fēng kǒu fèi** (*fung koe fay*)

Hush money.

非法集资 **fēifǎ jízī** (*fay fah gee dz*)

Ponzi scheme.

盗车贼 **dào chē zéi** (*daow chuh dzay*)

Motor vehicle theft. Literally "car stealer."

贩毒 **fàndú** (*fahn do*)

Trafficking/smuggling drugs. Literally "selling drugs."

毒枭 **dúxiāo** (*doo shaow*)

Drug lord.

黑 **hēi** (*hay*)

In Chinese anything illegal is called "black," or **hēi**. Thus the black market is the 黑市 **hēishì** (*hay shih*) (the literal meaning is the same as the English); an illegal cab is a 黑车 **hēichē** (*hay chuh*), literally "black car"; cooking the books results in a 黑单 **hēidān** (*hay dahn*), literally "black accounting"; a bad call in sports or an unfair decision by a judge, who may or may not have been bribed, is a 黑哨 **hēishào** (*hay shaow*), literally "black whistle"; and any sort of misdeed is a 黑点 **hēidiǎn** (*hay dyinn*), literally "black spot."

黑道 **hēidào** (*hay dow*)

Criminal gang. Literally "black path."

黑社会 **hēishèhuì** (*hay shuh hway*)

Mafia. Literally "black society."

三合会 **sān hé huì** (*sahn hay hway*)

Triad, the largest organized crime network in China. The Triads originally started out in the 1760s as a resistance movement to overthrow the Manchu emperor and restore Han Chinese rule. Their name, **sān hé huì**, literally means "three harmonies society," referring to the unity between heaven, earth, and man. After the Qing dynasty finally collapsed in 1911, these former outlaws and rebels, no longer enjoying the benefit of public support and funding, turned to crime and extortion to support themselves. Today there are thought to be as many as sixty separate Triad groups in Hong Kong alone, with membership of each one ranging anywhere from fifty to thirty thousand people, and more groups throughout Taiwan, Macao, mainland China, and around the world in cities with large overseas-Chinese communities like San Francisco, Los Angeles, New York, Philadelphia, Seattle, Boston, Miami, Chicago, Houston, Atlanta, Calgary, Vancouver, São Paulo, Melbourne, and Sydney.

涉黑 **shèhēi** (*shuh hay*)
Gang-related crimes.

人口贩卖 **rénkǒu fànmài** (*ren koe fahn my*)
Human trafficking. Literally "person selling."

蛇头 **shétóu** (*shuh toe*)
Snakehead. Someone (usually a gang member from Fujian Province) who smuggles illegal immigrants out of China and into other countries for a fee.

绑架 **bǎngjià** (*bahng jah*)
Kidnapping, abduction.

人口拐卖 **rénkǒu guǎimài** (*ren koe gwhy my*)
Human slavery. Literally "person abducting."

恶性伤人 **èxìng shāngrén** (*uh sheeng shahng ren*)
Aggravated assault.

杀人 **shārén** (*shah ren*)
Homicide. Literally "kill person."

谋杀 **móushā** (*moe shah*)
Murder. Literally "plan kill."

暗杀 **ànshā** (*ahn shah*)
Assassination. Literally "secret kill."

连环杀手 **liánhuánshāshǒu** (*lyinn hwun shah show*)
Serial killer. Literally "connected-ring kill hand."

食人 **shírén** (*shih ren*)
Cannibalism. Literally "eat people."

CHAPTER EIGHT

Internet Slang

In a country without a free press, it is impossible to overstate the profound impact that the Internet has had on society. The simple ability to see and read the internal thoughts of one's fellow compatriots, as well as the viewpoints of people from around the world, is prodding an estimated 250 million Chinese to express themselves more freely, to consider a multiplicity of opinions in matters of public debate, and, most simply, to feel just a little bit less alone in this world. And sure, the Internet is censored in China, but the efforts of government watchdogs can be best likened, as one well-known Chinese blogger put it, to a dam that "is leaking all over the place."

Online bulletin board systems (BBS) hosted by Chinese universities have long been hotbeds of intellectual debate, and today seemingly every company, media outlet, Web portal, and random organization in the country has a BBS garnering an estimated ten million new posts each day, with single posts frequently provoking hundreds, if not thousands, of replies. A mostly dead medium in the West, BBSs are invaluable to Chinese users because of the anonymity they afford. Blogs, too, are a noteworthy phenomenon, arguably far more widespread and vibrant than in the West. Everyone in China and their mother, it seems, has a blog: pop stars, CEOs of top companies, small-town mayors, powerful government officials, poor migrant workers, and journalists disillusioned with the censorship they face in their day jobs with state-owned media outlets. Many consider BBSs and blogs to be the truest reflection of what ordinary people on the ground really think about an issue—to the extent that the traditional media regularly quote from bloggers, and newspapers publish entire blog entries as op-ed columns.

There is, of course, a negative for every positive, and thus in the worst cases the Internet has served to ignite a terrifying mob mentality that hearkens back to the horrors of the Cultural Revolution. The "human-flesh search engine," as these "netizens" call themselves, is infamous for harnessing the power of the Internet to hunt down people who, deservedly or not, have been slandered online and deemed worthy of punishment by the online lynch mobs. Some people have been physically attacked; others have had to change addresses, jobs, and phone numbers. In one fairly typical example, a Chinese student attending Duke University, who was perceived to be in support of Free Tibet protestors, was targeted by angry Chinese who posted her picture, contact information, and parents' home address online. She received an avalanche of death threats, her parents got harassing phone calls at work, and one person claimed to have left human feces on her parents' doorstep.

Overall, however, the Internet's influence has been overwhelmingly positive. In many instances, it has filled in for the lack of a reliable judicial system and overcome endemic government corruption to bring justice for the masses. The Internet enables news of wrongdoing and injustice to spread at the speed of light and has spurred many real-life protests, petition drives, and heartfelt movements to get corrupt officials fired and persuade the central government to investigate allegations ignored by local governments. It has helped draw attention to corporate abuse and to raise money for ordinary people suffering under the weight of crippling medical costs and other hardships.

Not to imply, of course, that nascent revolution lurks in every bored instant message sent from one underpaid office worker to another, or every inane blog post about what some person ate for breakfast. Like Internet users the world over, Chinese netizens are chain-smoking in twenty-four-hour Internet cafés or lazing about at home, mainly idling away the days of their lives watching online video clips of stupid pet tricks, shopping for handbags on the Chinese equivalent to eBay, bitching about China's notoriously terrible national soccer team, and playing hour after interminable hour of Counter-Strike. And, hell, they may all know how to get around the government's censoring mechanisms, but, let's face it, the vast majority of them are doing so in order to download pirated movies and, of course, to watch porn.

So here, for your reference, is all the latest in chat slang, Internet crazes, and weirdo sociological phenomena that make up the vibrant, silly, important, ridiculous, and revolutionary world of the Chinese Internet.

Society, censorship, and Internet memes

GFW

Stands for "Great Firewall of China," a play on the Great Wall of China, and referring to China's Net Nanny, or Internet censoring mechanism.

河蟹 héxiè (*huh shih*)

Literally "river crab." A euphemism for Internet censorship. One of the main guiding philosophies of the Communist party is that of a "harmonious society," a catchphrase frequently played upon, parodied, and ironically referenced on the Internet. Using the word "censorship" will often get your site flagged by Web hosts, so when a post, or an entire Web site, gets blocked or deleted, Chinese Internet users sarcastically say that it's been "harmonized." "Harmony" in Chinese, 和谐 héxié (*huh shih*) is similar in pronunciation to "river crab." And since these euphemistic mentions of harmonization have become so ubiquitous that they themselves have become target keywords for getting censored, the Chinese have turned to "river crab" to stand in for harmonization.

功夫网 **gōngfu wǎng** (*gohng foo wahng*)

A euphemism for censorship. Literally "kung fu Web," but as with "river crab," mentions of kung fu in blog posts often refer to censorship. You'll notice that the pinyin **gōngfu wǎng** starts with *g*, *f*, and *w*. GFW is the abbreviation for the Great Firewall.

草泥马 **cǎonímǎ** (*tsow nee mah* – **cǎo** rhymes with "cow")

Grass mud horse. A made-up creature that has become an Internet sensation spawning everything from dolls to YouTube videos to scholarly essays because its otherwise benign name sounds like the obscenity 操你妈 **cào nǐ mā** (*tsow nee ma*), meaning "Fuck you," and because it has become a symbol of the fight against Internet censorship. The most popular online video about the creature, a parody of kiddie songs sung by a chipper chorus of children's voices, explains that the grass mud horse lives in the 马勒戈壁 **mǎlè gēbì** (*mah luh guh bee*), which innocently looks like "The Ma Le Desert" but sounds just like 妈了个屄 **mālegebī** (*mah luh guh bee*), or "your mother's a cunt." Moreover, the grass mud horse is often threatened by river crabs (a euphemism for Internet censorship, see the **héxiè** entry on page 157). While a phenomenon that involves children's voices singing "fuck you" and stick-figure online cartoons and dolls may seem juvenile, it neatly encapsulates the biggest issues surrounding the Chinese Internet. The authorities go on "anti-smut" campaigns to wipe out "inappropriate" material from the

Internet; netizens come up with clever ways to evade the censors, like saying "grass mud horse" instead of "fuck you," and maybe the censors start censoring the euphemism itself; but then netizens simply find yet another way to talk about the banned term or banned ideas, much the way "harmony" was used as a euphemism for "censorship" and then got censored, which spawned "river crab" in place of "harmony." And in the end, it becomes clear that any attempt to censor this unwieldy beast is a losing battle.

五毛党 wǔ máo dǎng (*ooh maow dahng*)

Literally "half-yuan party." People paid to influence Internet discussion by writing blog and BBS posts extolling the government's position on various issues and also to write comments in response to other posts, arguing the government's side of things. The payment structure for these people varies, but at the time this term was coined, the Hunan Province government was said to be paying a lump sum of six hundred yuan (around eighty or ninety dollars) plus an extra **wǔ máo** (half a yuan, about seven cents) per post.

ZF

Short for 政府 zhèngfǔ (*jung foo*), which means "government." ZF is often used in place of the Chinese characters so as not to attract the attention of the government censoring mechanism, which can be triggered by sensitive keywords.

JC

Stands for 警察 jǐngchá (*jeeng cha*), which means "police" or "police officer."

FB

Stands for 腐败 **fǔbaì** (*foo buy*). Means "corruption" in Chinese, and since corrupt officials are often wined and dined, people now ironically say **fǔbaì** to refer to going out to a fancy restaurant, going on vacation, or otherwise treating oneself to something nice.

FZL or 非主流 **fēizhǔliú** (*fay joo lew*— **liú** rhymes with "pew")

An "alternative" or "counterculture" person, usually rebellious and young with some sort of extreme style—elaborate hairstyle, piercings, unusual and edgy clothes, etc.—probably involving a great deal of influence from Japanese pop culture.

FQ or 愤青 **fènqīng** (*fen cheeng*)

Angry youth, patriotic youth. Coined in Hong Kong during the 1970s to refer to young people agitating for reform in Chinese society, but now used on the Internet to refer to extremely patriotic (or depending on your view of them, nationalistic) Chinese with aggressive stances on a number of political issues. Very broadly speaking, **fènqīng** tend to be virulently anti-Japanese and militantly opposed to Taiwanese and Tibetan independence. The issues at stake are complicated, and **fènqīng** attitudes can seem contradictory to anyone not familiar with their nuances. They often seem to unconditionally defend anything the Chinese government does but are simultaneously highly critical of that government for what they feel is too soft a stance on the core issues mentioned above. And they may exhibit intense xenophobia and call westernized Chinese "race traitors" while also believing that China should eventually democratize. Critics of **fènqīng** derogatorily call them 粪青 **fènqīng** (*fen cheeng*), a play on words that is pronounced the same as **fènqīng** but means "shit youth," or just 粪 **fènfèn** (*fen fen*): "shit."

人肉搜索 **rén ròu sōusuǒ** (*ren roe so swuh*)

Literally "human flesh search engine." Refers to the phenomenon of Internet users hunting down people in real life.

草根网民 **cǎogēn wǎngmín** (*tsow gehn wahng meeng*)

Self-described ordinary citizens (in mainland China) who generally don't have much of a voice, but who are slowly discovering the power of the Internet in helping to bring about social change (mainly in less sensitive areas like environmental protection, animal rights, labor rights, property rights, and rights for the disabled. Certain areas, however, cannot be touched without suffering consequences, such as attempting to organize politically). Literally "grassroots netizens" (a translation from the English).

晒黑族 **shaìhēi zú** (*shy hay dzoo*)

Literally "those who expose injustice." It refers to people on the Chinese mainland who use the Internet to help expose or publicize injustice: for example by mass blogging about an incident on many different Web servers in order to overcome possible online censorship. Every Web host seems to have different censoring criteria, and thus something that gets blocked or deleted on one host server may not get censored on another.

别太 CNN **bié tài CNN** (*byih tie CNN*)

Literally "don't be too CNN," meaning don't lie or distort the truth. When antigovernment rioting broke out in Lhasa in 2008, a perceived pro-Tibet, anti-China bias in Western media coverage provoked a rising tide of nationalism and anger among many Chinese. Someone started a Web site called Anti-CNN.com, with the slogan "Don't be too CNN!" and dedicated to showing examples of truth distortion in the Western media's China reporting. For example, one of the most hotly disputed photos, taken from the CNN Web site, portrayed two Tibetan men running away from Chinese military trucks rumbling ominously into town, but Anti-CNN posted the uncropped version of the photo that showed a group of Tibetan rioters throwing stones at the vehicles. Anger about media bias centers on CNN in particular because not long after the riots the CNN commentator Jack Cafferty outraged the public by referring to the Chinese as "a bunch of goons and thugs" during an on-air discussion about Chinese imports to the United States. Several (extremely dirty, profanity-filled) Chinese rap songs about the evils of "being too CNN" are also circulating on the Internet.

树洞贴 **shù dòng tiē** (*shoo dohng tyih*)

Literally "tree-hole post." The Wong Kar Wai movie *In the Mood for Love* closes with the protagonist traveling to the remains of an ancient temple in Cambodia, finding a small hole among the ruins, and whispering into it. The scene is based on a (perhaps made-up) saying that in the past, people would find a small hole in a tree, hide a secret in it, and then seal the hole with mud, to be kept hidden forever. In online parlance, **shù dòng tiē** refers to a popular trend of posting secrets anonymously on the Internet—anything ranging from one's salary to marital problems and beyond. People who do this are called 晒密族 **shaìmì zú** (*shy me dzoo*), literally "secret revealers," or 晒客族 **shaìkè zú**, literally "information exhibitionists."

我出来打酱油的 **wǒ chūlaí dǎ jiàngyóu de** (*wuh choo lie dah jyung yo duh*)

Literally, "I'm just out buying soy sauce." This phrase, along with "soy sauce guy," swept the Chinese Internet by storm thanks to a widely viewed Guangzhou TV news clip of a reporter asking an average man on the street his opinion of the latest celebrity scandal. The man famously replied "关我屌事, 我出来打酱油的" **"Guān wǒ diǎo shì, wǒ chūlai dǎ jiàngyóu de"** (*gwun wuh dyow shih, wuh choo lie dah jyung yo duh*)—"I don't give a shit, I'm just out buying soy sauce." Internet users have taken up the phrase "buying soy sauce" as a cynical euphemism for "It's none of my business" or "Who gives a fuck?" On the Chinese version of Facebook and other popular sites, one now commonly finds, among the possible answers to online polls, "I'm just buying soy sauce."

酱油男 **jiàngyóu nán** (*jahng yo nahn*)

Soy sauce guy. Indicating someone who ignores stupid shit.

很黄,很暴力 **hěn huáng, hěn bàolì** (*hun hwahng, hun baow lee*)

Literally "very yellow [pornographic], very violent." This phrase became all the rage because of a news broadcast on CCTV (China Central Television, which is state owned and thus considered a government tool) about government regulation of the Internet. A thirteen-year-old girl being interviewed about her impression of the Internet used the phrase to describe what she had ostensibly seen online. Chinese Internet users have mockingly taken up the phrase and now use it in all sorts of different contexts, or simply use the same sentence structure and substitute different adjectives besides "yellow" and "violent" to fit whatever they are talking about.

别太 CCTV **bié tài CCTV** (*byih tie CCTV*)

Don't be too CCTV. Meaning don't bullshit or be a tool or espouse propaganda. Came about after the 很黄,很暴力 **hěn huáng, hěn bàolì** incident (previous entry) on China's state-owned TV station.

很傻,很天真 **hěn shǎ, hěn tiānzhēn** (*hun shah, hun tyinn jen*)

Literally "very foolish, very naive." This phrase became popular after Hong Kong pop star Gillian Chung said it during a news conference. She was apologizing after pictures of her having sex with another celebrity, Edison Chen, were exposed on the Internet. Chinese Internet users were amused because it of its similarity to 很黄,很暴力 **hěn huáng, hěn bàolì** (page 163).

做俯卧撑 **zuò fǔwòchēng** (*dzwuh foo wuh chung*)

Literally "do push-ups" and a euphemism for a lame excuse or feelings of apathy. Stems from a June 2008 incident when the drowned body of a fifteen-year-old girl was found in Guizhou Province. The "push-up" reference comes from the provincial government's official statement about what happened, which in addition to not being believed by most netizens, included the bizarrely specific detail that one of the last people to see the girl alive, a friend of her boy-friend, started doing push-ups near her on a bridge and that "on the third one" she cried out and then jumped. Net-izens latched on to the detail, and sarcastic allusions to do-ing push-ups have flooded the Internet ever since. It generally means "it's none of my business," with a cynical edge that points to the futility of caring about anything when you are powerless to change things, but is sometimes used more lightheartedly to suggest a feeble excuse. "What were you doing in a sex chat room anyway?" "Uh . . . I was just doing push-ups."

节约点, 喝茅台 **jiéyuē diǎn, hē Máotái** (*jyih yreh dyinn, huh maow tie*)

This catchphrase, which means "economize: drink Moutai," comes from a report about a government official in Sichuan Province who beat up a shopkeeper for charging him too much for a bottle of Moutai (a high-end brand of Chinese liquor). It was explained that "Director Cao wanted to economize, because money is tight at the personnel bureau and he still owes money for house repairs." The irony of this statement was not lost on Chinese netizens, and this quickly became the newest Internet meme, as Moutai is strongly as-sociated with government corruption (no shady deal is sealed without a booze-soaked dinner involving copious amounts of this expensive liquor).

恶搞 **ègǎo** (*uh gow*)

An umbrella term for China's Internet parody culture (in-cluding online videos and Photoshop images spoofing cur-rent events). Literally "evil doings" or "restless work." It

comes from the Japanese word *kuso*, which spread first to
Taiwan and then throughout greater China. *Kuso* means
"shit" and also "poor quality" and described a Japanese fad
for appreciating shitty computer games (similar to when we
call a movie "so bad it's good"). Since these terrible computer games were often unintentionally funny, in Taiwan the
meaning eventually shifted to include anything ridiculous or
funny.

网友 **wǎngyǒu** (*wahng yo*)

Internet friend(s). Making friends via the Internet is much,
much more common in China than in the West. Westerners
chatting online in China are often startled by the large number of messages they receive from Chinese strangers who are
just searching for new friends to chat with. Some of these
Internet friends are simply people to chat with while idling
away the hours at work, some meet up in person, and some
start relationships. Some Chinese even meet people by tex-
ting random phone numbers in the hopes of happening
upon someone friendly.

网瘾 **wǎngyǐn** (*wahng een*)

Internet addiction. In 2008 China became the first country
in the world to officially recognize this as a clinical disorder,
similar to alcoholism and compulsive gambling, after several
well-publicized cases in which young people died after
spending days or weeks glued to the computer screen in
Internet cafés. The country has several officially licensed
Internet addiction clinics and has also seen a spate of unli-
censed, hidden Internet cafés where kids banned from the
Internet by their parents secretly go to play games.

Emoticons and expressions

颜文字 **yán wénzì** (*yen when dz*)

Emoticon. Literally "face character."

凸

In normal written Chinese, this is the character 凸 **tū** (*too*), meaning "convex." It is frequently used on the Internet as an emoticon, however, because it looks like a hand giving the middle finger.

Orz

Meant to look like a person kneeling on the ground, on hands and knees, with head bowed—the *O* is the person's head, *r* is the arm and torso, and *z* is the bent leg. Used to express shock, hopelessness, frustration, despondence, or, more positively, respect or awe—basically any emotion that might be suggested by a kneeling figure.

A few variations (among many) include:

szQ (Orz kneeling in the opposite direction and licking the floor)

Oroz (Orz with a fat stomach)

囧

An emoticon indicating sadness, frustration, shock, or amusement. The character 囧 **jiǒng** (*jyohng*—the *o* sound is long), which dates back to ancient times, originally meant "bright" but has taken on this new meaning because it looks like a sad face (or a shocked or amused face, depending on your interpretation). "**Jiǒng** culture" has taken off as a full-

fledged fad that has spilled over into real life—the character can even be found on T-shirts, bags, and other accessories.

A few variations (of many) include:

商 (**jiǒng** wearing a bamboo hat)

d 囧 b (**jiǒng** with a thumbs-up on either side of its face, from a Pepsi marketing campaign called "Love China")

囧rz (Orz combined with **jiǒng**, so that the kneeling person has a **jiǒng** face)

槑 **meí** (*may*)

Stupefied, shocked. This obscure character dates back to ancient times and means "plum." It is made of two characters for 呆 **dāi** (*die*) next to each other, and since 呆 alone can mean something like "dumb" or "astounded" or "foolish," having two next to each other doubles the degree.

雷 **leí** (*lay*)

Literally "thunder." Used to indicate shock or surprise or outrage (or any emotion that might be represented by the image of someone being thunderstruck). Moreover, on both the Internet and in real life 雷人 **léirén** (*lay ren*), literally "thunder person," has come to mean "outrageous" or "shocking" or "absurd." One especially common expression is 太雷人了 **tài léirén le** (*tie lay ren luh*), meaning "too outrageous" or "that's so stupid" or "that's insane."

汗 **hàn** (*hahn*)

Means "sweat" and is used, usually in reply, to indicate feeling embarrassed or dumbfounded (that is, an emotion that makes you sweat).

泪 **lèi** (*lay*)

Means "tear" or "teardrop" and used online to express sadness or crying.

晕 **yūn** (*een*)

Means "dizzy" or "faint" and is often used to express surprise, shock, amusement, or disgust; that is, emotions that might make you feel faint.

我倒 **wǒ dǎo** (*wuh daow*)

Literally, "I fall over." Used the same way as **yūn** (above).

VoV

Represents a person holding up two peace signs on either side of his or her face.

闪

The character 闪 **shǎn** (*shahn*) means "flash" and is used in online chatting to mean "leaving," as when you leave a chat room—you might say 我闪了 **wǒ shǎn le** (*wuh shahn luh*), "I'm leaving"—or "avoid doing something."

Insults and mockery

BS

Usually means the English "bullshit" but may also stand for 鄙视 **bǐshì** (*bee shih*), which literally means "despise."

JP

Stands for 极品 **jípǐn** (*gee peen*), literally "extreme conduct." Basically means "weirdo" or, rather, an eccentric or anyone who behaves unconventionally.

LB

Stands for 篱笆 **líbā** (*lee bah*), the name of an online forum (Liba) known for being popular among materialistic girls. Vapid, shallow girls, then, are often dismissively described as LB.

BC

Stands for 白痴 **báichī** (*buy chih*), or "idiot."

SL

Stands for 色狼 **sèláng** (*suh lahng*), or "pervert."

永久性脑残 **yǒngjǐu xìng nǎocán** (*yohng joe sheeng now tsahn*)

Literally means something like "permanent brain damage" and used to comment on someone or something you find weird or crazy.

小白 **xiǎobái** (*shaow buy*)

Layman, novice, someone with little knowledge about something (such as computers). Literally "little white." Refers to 白痴 **báichī** (*buy chih*), which means "idiot."

菜鸟 **càiniǎo** (*tsie nyow*—**cài** rhymes with "pie")

Newbie. Literally "food bird." Pigeons raised for food are of a lower class than homing pigeons, and thus the phrase is used to describe junior-level people in various fields.

国猪 **guózhū** (*gwuh joo*)

Literally "country's pigs" or "national pigs." An insulting pun on 国足 **guózú** (*gwuh dzoo*) (**zhū** and **zú** sound similar), which is the term for China's national soccer team—a target of much abuse among soccer fans due to its poor performance and frequently scandalous or embarrassing behavior. Speaking of which . . .

我是洗澡来的 **wǒ shì xǐzǎo laí dè** (*wuh shih she dzow lie duh*)

Literally, "I just came here to take a shower." Refers to a 2008 scandal when members of the Chinese national soccer team got caught checking into a hotel with a bunch of women who may or may not have been hookers. One of them protested by saying, "I just came here to take a shower." Now the phrase is often used as a euphemism for any feeble excuse.

恐龙 **kǒnglóng** (*kohng lohng*—like "Kong" and "long" but pronounced with a long *o*, or *oh*, sound)

Online slang for an ugly girl. Literally "dinosaur."

青蛙 **qīngwā** (*ching wah*)

Online slang for an ugly guy. The counterpart to "dinosaur" (above). Literally means "frog."

拍砖 **paīzhuān** (*pie jwahn*)

Literally means "smack with a brick." Used online when strongly criticizing someone or something. For example, you might say 请拍砖 **qǐng pāizhuān** (*ching pie jwahn*), literally "please smack with a brick," to mean "prove it"; or 我拍砖 **wǒ pāizhuān** (*wuh pie jwahn*), literally "I smack with a brick," to mean "here's what I think."

Dirty/lewd/slangy

牛 **niú** (*nyoo*)

Literally means "cow" and used to call someone or something "awesome." Short for **niúbī** (see chapter 1), which means "fuckin' awesome."

NB

Stands for 牛屄 **niúbī** (*nyoo bee*), which can negatively mean something like "cocky bastard" or positively refer to a dar-ing, impressive person or thing—someone or something that is "fuckin' badass" (see chapter 1). Is also frequently written using the character 牛 plus any other Chinese character pronounced *bee*, such as 逼 **bī**, "to force," or 比 **bǐ**, an indication of comparison. The real character 屄 **bī** (*bee*) cannot be typed on most computers and thus is almost never used.

装 B

Stands for 装屄 **zhuāngbī** (*jwahng bee*), which means "fucking poser" or "fake motherfucker." 装 **Zhuāng** (*jwahng*) means "pretend" and **bī** indicates **niúbī** (see previous entry and chapter 1), meaning "fucking badass." Thus the term implies that you are pretending to be badass. Some online users write "IB" or "install B" instead because **zhuāng** can also mean "install."

SB or 傻 B

Stands for 傻屄 **shǎbī** (*shah bee*), which means something like "stupid cunt" or "motherfucker." Literally "idiot's pussy." Also frequently written 傻逼 **shǎbī** or 傻比 **shǎbǐ**; that is, substituting a similar-sounding character for 屄.

TMD

Stands for 他妈的 **tāmāde** (*ta ma duh*), literally "his mother's," implying "fuck his mother's pussy." A moderately strong curse word. Sometimes shortened to MD, for 妈的 **māde** (*ma duh*), literally "mother's."

Some of these abbreviations can be combined, for example, TMDSB stands for 他妈的傻 B **tāmāde shǎbī** (*ta ma duh shah bee*), which is equivalent to saying something like "fucking stupid" or "stupid-ass shit" or "goddamn stupid cunt."

NND or TNND

Stands for 奶奶的 **nǎinai de** (*nigh nigh duh*) or 他奶奶的 **tā nǎinai de** (*ta nigh nigh duh*). Literally "grandmother's" or "his grandmother's" and implies the larger phrase "fuck your grandmother." However, this fragment alone means something slightly less profane, closer to "shit" or "damn."

QQXX

Stands for 我圈圈你个叉叉 **wǒ quān quān nǐ gè chā chā** (*wuh chren chren nee guh cha cha*), a euphemistic way of saying "fuck you." 圈 **Quān** (*chren*), literally "circle," refers to a penis here, while 叉 **chā** (*cha*), literally "cross," refers to pussy. Literally, it means "I circle your cross."

G8 or JB

Means "dick" or "cock." In the first case, because *G* and the number eight in Chinese, **bā** (*bah*), it sounds like 鸡巴 **jība** (*gee bah*), which is a slang term for "dick." The second is just an abbreviation based on the first letters of the pinyin syllables in **jība**.

JJ

Stands for 鸡鸡 **jījī** (*gee gee*), a kiddie term for "penis," like "wee-wee." Can also stand for 姐姐 **jiějie** (*jyih jyih*), which means "older sister" and refers to any female who is older than the person addressing her, though generally still a young woman.

SY

Stands for 手淫 **shǒuyín** (*show een*), which means "jerk off" (verb).

GC

Stands for 高潮 **gāocháo** (*gaow chow*), which means "orgasm," "climax," "come."

JY

Stands for 精液 **jīngyè** (*jing yeh*), which means "semen," "sperm," or "ejaculate."

YY

Stands for 意淫 **yìyín** (*ee een*) and means something like "to have pervy thoughts" or "think dirty" but can also have a less negative connotation that just indicates thinking or behaving unconventionally or creatively.

YD

Short for 淫荡 **yíndàng** (*een dahng*), meaning "lascivious" or "lewd."

More abbreviations and language play

PP

Can mean, variously, 漂漂 **piāopiao** (*pyow pyow*), "pretty"; 片片 **piànpian** (*pyinn pyinn*), "picture"; or 屁屁 **pìpi** (*pee pee*), "butt." Thus someone could conceivably write, "I've seen her PP. She's not very PP, but she's got a nice PP."

MM

Stands for 妹妹 **meìmeì** (*may may*), which literally means "little sister" but can generally refer to a girl or young woman. Use carefully, however, as it can also refer more euphemistically to a woman's own "little sister"; i.e., her vagina. Can also stand for 美眉 **měiméi** (*may may*), which derives from **meìmeì** but is written with different characters that instead mean "beautiful eyebrow" and is slang for a pretty girl. Along these same lines, you'll also see abbreviations for all the other types of people you might be talking about online: LG for 老公 **lǎogōng** (*laow gohng*), "husband"; LP for 老婆 **lǎopó** (*laow pwuh*), "wife"; GG for 哥哥 **gēge** (*guh guh*), "older brother" or any older male; JM or JMs for 姐妹们 **jiěmèimen** (*jyih may men*), "sisters"; and DD for 弟弟 **dìdi** (*dee dee*), "little brother" or any younger male. However, MM is the most common abbreviation you'll see, given that the overwhelming majority of Chinese Internet users are male and, of course, endlessly preoccupied with MM.

ML

Make love.

PMP

Stands for 拍马屁 **paīmǎpì** (*pie mah pee*), literally "pat the horse's butt," and means to flatter or suck up to someone.

汗语 **hànyǔ** (*hahn yee*)

Chat room jargon, Internet slang. A play on 汉语 **hànyǔ** (*hahn yee*), which is pronounced exactly the same but means Mandarin Chinese. The only difference is that 汉 **hàn** (*hahn*) is replaced with the character for "sweat," 汗 **hàn** (*hahn*), which is itself online jargon for feeling embarrassed, shocked, or frustrated.

51.com

"I want" dot com. "Five one" in Chinese is **wǔ yào** (*wooh yow*—which might not make sense if you're familiar with the Taiwanese pronunciation, "one" is usually pronounced **yī** (*eee*), but mainland Chinese usually say **yào** instead of **yī** when saying the number out loud). **Wǔ yào** sounds a bit like the Chinese for "I want," 我要 **wǒ yào** (*wuh yow*). So many Chinese URLs begin with the number fifty-one. Hence there is a job-search site with the URL www.51job.com (i.e., I want a job), and a credit card consultancy with the URL www.51credit.com (I want credit).

88

Bye-bye. The number eight in Chinese is **bā** (*bah*), which sounds to Chinese ears like the English word "bye." Another variation is 886, **bā bā liù** (*bah bah lew*—the last syllable rhymes with "ew"), and is similar to 拜拜喽 **bàibài lóu** (*bye bye low*), which also means "bye-bye."

555

The sound of crying. The number five in Chinese is **wǔ** (*wooh*), which sounds like 呜 **wū** (*ooh*), an onomatopoeic word for humming or crying. Thus 呜呜呜, or 555, represents the sound of someone crying. Insert as many fives as you deem necessary to adequately represent the volume of your tears.

3Q

Thank you. The number three in Chinese is **sān** (*sahn*) and combined with the English letter *Q* (*sahn-cue*) sounds to Chinese ears like "thank you."

3X

Thank you. X refers to 谢谢 **xièxiè** (*shih shih*), which is the Chinese for "thank you."

NoQ

You're welcome. It doesn't make sense aurally but is based on 3Q (above), meaning "thank you."

520

I love you. "Five two zero" in Chinese is **wǔ èr líng** (*oo er ling*), which sounds somewhat similar to 我爱你 **wǒ ài nǐ** (*wuh aye nee*), the Chinese for "I love you."

1314

Means "forever" because the pronunciation of "one three one four" in Chinese, **yī sān shí sì** (*ee sahn ee sih*), sounds similar to 一生一世 **yīshēng yī shì** (*ee shung ee shih*), which means "forever." Most commonly used in expressions of love, in particular 5201314; i.e., "I love you forever" (see above).

8147

Stands for 不要生气 **bù yào shēngqì** (*boo yow shung chee*), "don't be angry," because they sound similar—as do the following:

360

想念你 **Xiǎngniàn nǐ** (*shyahng nyinn nee*), "miss you."

246

饿死了 **É sǐ le** *(uh sih luh)*, "I'm hungry."

7456

气死我了 **Qìsǐwǒle** (*chee sih wuh luh*), "I'm so angry!"

GL

Short for "girl love," referring to lesbians or lesbianism.

BL

Short for "boy love," referring to gay men or homosexuality.

MF

Stands for 麻烦 **máfan** (*ma fun*), meaning "trouble" or "hassle."

TAXI

Stands for 太可惜 **tài kěxī** (*tie kuh she*), meaning "what a pity" or "that sucks."

FL

Stands for 发廊 **fàláng** (*fah lahng*), or "hair salon," referring to prostitutes who work under the guise of a hairdresser. Hair salons in China that are actually brothels are usually (usually) recognizable by their pink lighting.

粉丝 **fěnsī** (*fen sih*)

Literally "vermicelli" (a type of noodle) but used online to mean "fans" because it sounds similar. Other variants include just 粉 **fěn** (*fen*) by itself and 饭 **fàn** (*fahn*), literally "rice" or "meal."

摸我 **mō wǒ** (*mwuh wuh*)

Literally means, "touch me." Used to say "MSN me" (i.e., chat me via MSN). MSN's instant messaging service is immensely popular in China, and the first letter of MSN sounds to Chinese ears like the word 摸 **mō** (*mwuh*), which means "touch."

得体 **détǐ** (*duh tee*)

Literally means "good and proper," but because it sounds like the English word "dirty," which has the opposite meaning, the word has been punned on and joked about to the extent that it has now taken on the alternate meaning of "someone who seems good on the outside but is actually bad on the inside." This new usage has been popularized by the song "Dirty" by Taiwanese-American singer Lee-Hom Wang.

Praise

BT

Stands for 变态 **biàntài** (*byinn tie*), which means "perverted" or "deviant" and once referred to homosexuality, sexual fetishes, people with an abnormal fixation on violence, etc. In

online culture, however, it has now taken on a joking or positive connotation; thus calling someone BT is akin to cheer-
fully saying something like "you pervert" or "you weirdo" to
a friend, or like saying "you're so bad" when what you really
mean is that you're impressed.

PF

Stands for 佩服 **pèifú** (*pay foo*), meaning "admire."

赞 **zàn** (*dzahn*)

Means "to praise" and is often used online when recom-
mending or raving about a movie, a story, etc.

94

Agreed, I agree. "Nine four" in Chinese is **jǐu sì** (*joe sih*),
which sounds like the phrase 就是 **jiùshì** (*joe shih*), which
means "yes" or "it's true."

PL

Stands for 漂亮 **piàoliàng** (*pyow lyahng*), or "pretty."

PPMM

Stands for 漂漂妹妹 **piàopiào mèimèi** (*pyow pyow may may*),
a cutesy way of saying "pretty girl."

ML

Stands for 美丽 **měilì** (*may lee*), or "beautiful."

Miscellaneous

火星文 **huǒxīngwén** (*hwuh sheeng when*)

Internet or text-messaging shorthand, such as "lol," "Cul8r," and "b4." Literally "martian language" because the hodge-podge use of numbers, symbols, made-up words, and letters from other languages looks like a new, foreign (or inter-planetary, thus martian) language.

火星人 **huǒxīngrén** (*hwuh sheeng ren*)

A martian. That is, someone out of touch with reality or with the latest news and trends. A commenter might jokingly (or pejoratively) reply to such a person, "你是火星回来的吗?" **"Nǐ shì huǒxīng huílai de ma?"** (*nee shih hwuh sheeng hway lie duh ma*): "Did you just get back from Mars?" In general, Chinese Internet users frequently make jokes about being from Mars in response to things they find funny or bizarre.

火星贴 **huǒxīng tiē** (*hwuh sheeng tyih*)

Literally "post from Mars." Refers to an extremely old post. If someone posts something old that everyone's seen before, someone might comment, "This is a post from Mars."

LZ

Stands for 楼主 **lóuzhǔ** (*low joo*), which refers to the author of a post or the person who starts a BBS thread. So you might write something like, "I agree with LZ." Literally means "building owner" or "owner of the house."

沙发 **shāfā** (*shah fa*)

Literally means "sofa" and refers to the first person to reply to a post. Since LZ (page 182) is the "owner of the house," the first person to reply, or enter the house, gets the sofa. Sometimes just written in English, as "sofa." The next commenter after the "sofa" is referred to as 坐板凳 **zuò bǎndèng** (*zwuh bahn dung*), meaning "sitting on a bench."

高楼 **gāolóu** (*gaow low*)

Literally means "tall building" and used online to refer to a topic or post that attracts hundreds of replies, making the thread taller and taller, like a high-rise building.

斑竹 **bānzhú** (*bahn joo*)

Literally "bamboo" but used to refer to a BBS moderator because it is pronounced exactly like the real term for the moderator, which is 版主 **bānzhú** (*bahn joo*).

RT

Stands for 如题 **rútí** (*roo tee*), which means "refer to the title or subject." A common response when someone asks a stupid question, as in, "Look at the title and subject—the answer is obvious from that."

286

Out of fashion, out of date, old-fashioned. Refers to an old, and thus outdated, computer chip from the 1980s (the Intel 80286).

死机 **sǐjī** (*sih gee*)

Means "unexpected computer shutdown." Literally "dead machine," but now more widely used to indicate being so dumbfounded by something that you can't even respond.

蜜 **mì** (*me*) and 黑 **hēi** (*hay*)

Mì means "honey" and is tacked onto a word to indicate fervent support for a certain athlete or sports team, the way we might use "freak," as in "He's a total Raiders freak." **Hēi** means "black" and is used the same way, but to indicate hatred.

晒 **shài** (*shy*)

Literally means "to air" or "to sun" and can thus suggest "to show." Used online to refer to the popular phenomenon of netizens photographing their stuff (some women, for example, like to photograph their extensive and very expensive collection of cosmetics and beauty products) and posting the pictures online to show off, prompt discussions about favorite products, share recommendations, etc. Another common variation is 兽 **shòu** (*show*), which means "beast" but sounds exactly like the English word "show."

长草 **zhǎng cǎo** (*dzahng tsow*)

Literally "grow grass." On the Chinese Internet, feelings of yearning or want are described as "grass growing in the heart," and netizens often use the expression when they see things they want that other netizens **shài** or **shòu** (see above) online.

三手病 **sān shǒu bìng** (*sahn show bing*)

Literally "three hands illness." Describes tiredness of the hand due to excessive computer use. A person who spends too much time gaming or online is called a 三手 **sān shǒu** (*sahn show*). An equivalent Western concept might be "Blackberry thumb": pain caused by typing too much with your thumbs on your Blackberry.

假跳 **jiǎtiào** (*jah tyow*)

Used online to mean "lie." Literally "false jump." It comes from the role-playing computer game PK: Police and Killer, and it refers to when a policeman in the game pretends that he has mistaken a civilian for the killer.

爆头 **bàotóu** (*baow toe*)

Literally "explode head." This term comes from the computer game Counter-Strike, in which it refers to killing an opponent, but has spread beyond that context to mean any sort of unexpected attack or blow.

留爪 **liú zhuǎ** (*lyew jwa*—the first syllable rhymes with "ew")

Literally "leave a claw mark." Refers to posting on BBSs.

失写症 **shī xiě zhēng** (*shih shyih jung*)

Literally "lose writing illness." Refers to the phenomenon of using the computer so much that you forget how to write Chinese characters by hand.

凤凰男 **fènghuáng nán** (*fung hwahng nahn*)

Literally "phoenix man." A newly coined term for a 穷小子 **qióng xiǎozi** (*chyohng shyow dz*), or "poor guy," from a rural area whose family scrimps and saves to put him through school so he can go to the big city and find a job. His success is analogized to a rising phoenix.

孔雀女 **kǒngquè nǚ** (*kohng chreh nee*—the first syllable essentially rhymes with "cone" but with the same ending sound as "long")

A spoiled city girl who grew up with money. The counterpart to a "phoenix man" (above). Literally "peacock woman" and a newly coined term for a 富家女 **fùjiā nǚ** (*foo jah nee*), or "wealthy-family woman." Both "phoenix man" and "peacock woman" are often used as a kind of shorthand in discussions of the culture clash between young people from different backgrounds, a byproduct of China's rapid urbanization. Marriages between a "phoenix man" and "peacock woman," and their resultant problems, are an especially widely discussed issue.

草莓族 **cǎoméi zú** (*tsow may dzoo*)

A 草莓 **cǎoméi** (*tsow may*) is a strawberry and 族 **zú** (*dzoo*) means "race," "clan," or "generation"—basically any wide grouping of people. **Cǎoméi zú** is a slightly negative nickname for the younger generation (or the 80 后 **bāshíhòu** (*bah shih ho*), those born "after 1980"). Like the fruit, members of the "strawberry clan" are good-looking thanks to their youth, confidence, fashionable clothes, and the other trappings of a cushy life but are soft and easily bruised (that is, they don't hold up well under pressure) because they've had it easy all their lives.

榴莲族 **liúlián zú** (*lyoo lyinn dzoo*)

Durian clan. A durian is an indigenous Southeast Asian fruit with a tough, thorny husk, which is well-known mostly because it smells horrendous—enough so that it is banned on the subway in Singapore. It is perhaps this negative perception surrounding the fruit that has inspired younger people from the "strawberry clan" to give this moniker to what they consider the unprogressive and out-of-touch older generation.

椰子族 **yēzi zú** (*yeh dz dzoo*)

Coconut clan. A moniker for young people who are the opposite of the strawberry clan—able to work very hard and "eat bitterness" because of their tough husks. Why exactly Chinese seem to love categorizing people with names of fruits is unclear, but it means that bewildering comments like these are common on Internet forums: "Not just the strawberry generation, but the generation of children who will graduate college in 2010. How will they know how to face the world's realities? Strawberries will seem cactuses compared to what these delicate orchids will be once they are cast adrift on the seas of real life's waters."

山寨 **shānzhài** (*shahn jie—jie* rhymes with "die")

Literally "mountain stronghold," alluding to a period in China's history when various areas were controlled by renegade warlords (with mountain strongholds); that is, outside official control. Today **shānzhài** retains that renegade idea but means "knockoff" or "fake." It can also mean "inferior" or "cheap," though more recently the word has taken on a more positive connotation, suggesting ingenuity and a sense of humor, as people begin to embrace "**shānzhài** culture." Knockoff mobile phone makers extoll the **shānzhài** nature of their products, arguing that they are making high-end products accessible to the masses, and some companies even cheekily use **shānzhài** spokespeople—that is, celebrity look-alikes—to endorse their products. One especially hilarious example of **shānzhài** culture's tongue-in-cheek nature: KFC's Chinese name is 肯德基 **Kěn Dé Jī** (*ken duh gee*), but one **shānzhài** business, also serving fried chicken and fast food, calls itself 啃他鸡 **Kěn Tā Jī** (*ken tah gee*), which sounds similar but means "nibble his chicken" and is a dirty double entendre, since 鸡 **jī** (*gee*) is a slang term for "penis."

极品女 **jípǐn nǚ** (*gee peen nee*) and 极品男 **jípǐn nán** (*gee peen nahn*)

Literally "extremely great woman" and "extremely great man" but often used sarcastically on the Internet to mean someone who is fussy or annoying.

宅女 **zhái nǚ** (*jigh nee*) and 宅男 **zhái nán** (*jigh nahn*)

A woman or man, respectively, who stays indoors all day and spends all her or his time on the Internet. A Japanese slang term (written with the same characters) that spread first to Taiwan and is now frequently used by Internet users all over China.

The Top Twenty-five Terms You Need to Know

哇塞 **wā sài** (*wah sigh*) oh my god!

废话 **fèihuà** (*fay hwa*) nonsense!

放屁 **fàngpì** (*fahng pee*) bullshit!

白痴 **báichī** (*buy chih*) idiot

太雷人了 **tài léirén le** (*tie lay ren luh*) that's insane

酷 **kù** (*coo*) cool

牛 **niú** (*nyoo*) awesome

他妈的 **tāmāde** (*tah mah duh*) damn

我靠 **wǒ kào** (*wuh cow*) shit!

操你妈 **cào nǐ mā** (*tsow nee ma*) fuck you!

泡妞 **pàonīu** (*pow nyoo*) hit on girls

马子 **mǎzi** (*mah dz*) girlfriend

凯子 **kǎizi** (*kigh dz*) boyfriend

同志 **tóngzhì** (*tohng jih*) gay

鸡巴 **jība** (*gee bah*) dick

波波 **bōbō** (*bwuh bwuh*) boobs

吹箫 **chuīxiāo** (*chway shaow*) blow job

做爱 **zuò'ài** (*zwuh aye*) have sex

干 **gàn** (*gahn*) screw, fuck

打飞机 **dǎfēijī** (*dah fay gee*) jerk off, hand job

屄 **bī** (*bee*) pussy

傻屄 **shǎbī** (*shah bee*) stupid cunt

毛片 **máopiān** (*mao pyinn*) porno

鸡 **jī** (*gee*) prostitute

色狼 **sèláng** (*suh lahng*) pervert